ANTI-RACIST EDUCATIONAL LEADERSHIP AND POLICY

Anti-Racist Educational Leadership and Policy helps educational leaders better comprehend the racial implications and challenges of the current educational policy landscape. Each chapter unpacks a policy issue such as school choice, school closures, standardized testing, discipline, and school funding, and analyzes it through the racialized and market-driven lenses of the current leadership context. Full of real examples, this book equips aspiring school leaders with the skills to question how a policy addresses or fails to address racism, action-oriented strategies to develop anti-racist solutions, and the tools to encourage their school community to promote racial equity. This important book demystifies a complex policy context and prepares current and future teacher leaders, principals, and superintendents to lead their schools towards more equitable practice.

Sarah Diem is Associate Professor of Educational Leadership & Policy Analysis at the University of Missouri, USA.

Anjalé D. Welton is a professor in the Department of Educational Leadership and Policy Analysis at the University of Wisconsin–Madison, USA.

ANTI-RACIST EDUCATIONAL LEADERSHIP AND POLICY

ADDRESSING RACISM IN PUBLIC EDUCATION

Sarah Diem and Anjalé D. Welton

NEW YORK AND LONDON

First published 2021
by Routledge
52 Vanderbilt Avenue, New York, NY 10017

and by Routledge
2 Park Square, Milton Park, Abingdon, Oxon, OX14 4RN

Routledge is an imprint of the Taylor & Francis Group, an informa business

© 2021 Taylor & Francis

The right of Sarah Diem and Anjalé D. Welton to be identified as authors of this work has been asserted by them in accordance with sections 77 and 78 of the Copyright, Designs and Patents Act 1988.

All rights reserved. No part of this book may be reprinted or reproduced or utilized in any form or by any electronic, mechanical, or other means, now known or hereafter invented, including photocopying and recording, or in any information storage or retrieval system, without permission in writing from the publishers.

Trademark notice: Product or corporate names may be trademarks or registered trademarks, and are used only for identification and explanation without intent to infringe.

Library of Congress Cataloging-in-Publication Data
A catalog record for this title has been requested

ISBN: 978-1-138-59697-9 (hbk)
ISBN: 978-1-138-59699-3 (pbk)
ISBN: 978-0-429-48722-4 (ebk)

Typeset in New Baskerville
by Newgen Publishing UK

To our families—thank you for your love and unwavering support.

To the students, educators, administrators, families, organizers, and activists fighting for educational justice and racial equity every day across your school communities—we thank you for your passion, humanity, and commitment to creating an education system all students deserve.

Contents

Foreword   viii
H. RICHARD MILNER IV

Preface   xi

Acknowledgments   xiv

1 Anti-Racism and Color-Evasiveness in a Neoliberal Context: An Introduction   1

2 How School Leaders Respond to Demographic Change   23

3 School Choice and Who Has a Right to Choose   37

4 The Racial Politics of School Closure and Community Response   58

5 Standardized Testing and the Racial Implications of Data Use   80

6 School Funding and the Need for Resource Redistribution   97

7 Racism and School Discipline: From Schools to Prison, or Schools *As* a Prison   115

8 A Protocol for Anti-Racist Policy Decision-Making in Educational Leadership   138

Index   152

Foreword
H. Richard Milner IV

Recently, I was conducting a professional development session with a group of educators (school counselors, teachers, leaders, social workers, and so forth), and I asked them if elementary school teachers should teach anti-racism. Interestingly, the overall response among the educators in the room was that they would "address" and "respond to" racism if they "heard" some racist comment from a student or if they saw a group of students being "mean" to another student based on race. As I probed, in general, what I heard from the educators was, "I will address racism if I am forced to or in response to a particular situation." I was disappointed. What I tried to convey to the group of educators was that either they were working against racism, or they were working to maintain it.

Anti-Racist Educational Leadership and Policy: Addressing Racism in Public Education is an incredibly important book because it provides recommendations, tools, and insights about how school leaders and others build their anti-racist muscles in the fight for racial justice. By critiquing and calling out "common sense" policies and practices that have done more harm than good, Diem and Welton, drawing from empirical research, demonstrate what practitioners can do to transform their schools and build systems of racial equity.

There are no neutral spaces in the work of equity, racial justice, advocacy, and activism. Either we are working towards anti-racism or we are working against it. Either we are anti-xenophobia or we are maintaining xenophobia. Either we are anti-sexism or we are working to maintain sexism. But rather than focusing solely on what individual leaders and other educators can (and should) do to build their knowledge, understanding, insights, and expertise, this book is also about how to build policies that support institutional and structural spaces of equity and justice.

We are living in dangerously racist times. White supremacy, anti-Blackness, xenophobia, and hate are intensifying. Although such racism is not new, technological shifts and advancements provide us more opportunities to witness acts of discrimination in real time. Although some may believe issues of race are improving in the United States (U.S.), one could argue that we are regressing as a nation. Through technology, our ability to document and chronicle injustice provides opportunities for us to deepen what we know as well as engage in powerful dialogue about just how far we have (not) come in the U.S. in terms of race. White supremacist organizations are bolder, more vocal, and more overt in their racist attacks than they were years ago. The violent Unite the Right protests in Charlottesville, Virginia, and the subsequent killing of Heather Heyer provide a good example of white supremacy at work (https://time.com/after-charlottesville-ruddy-roye/). Moreover, racial divisiveness can be substantiated with the reactions to Colin Kaepernick's decision to exercise his right to kneel during the national anthem as a player in the national football league (Wagoner, 2016) to protest the police killing of unarmed Black people (https://theundefeated.com/features/colin-kaepernick-protests-anthem-over-treatment-of-minorities/). The Pittsburgh synagogue shooting where 11 were killed is another example (www.cnn.com/2018/10/28/us/pittsburgh-synagogue-shooting-victims/index.html). We also see an increase in media reports related to race as white people call law enforcement on Black people at appalling rates for seemingly mundane acts. Racism and xenophobia also manifest in immigrant children being confined to cages at the Mexican border, separated from their families for extended periods of time.

What roles should school leaders play in building school climates that address, disrupt, and build a proactive stance against the incidents described above? What is essential for educators to know, understand, and be able to do in order to cultivate curriculum practices in schools that center these societal injustices and incidents inside of school? Diem and Welton argue that schools must build systems through transformative ideologies to eradicate injustice. Moreover, these authors stress that the impact of equitable systems must move beyond the walls of the classroom and school. Anti-racism and advocacy, for educators and perhaps especially for school leaders, must be central to their stance in their work in schools, as Diem and Welton explain, in order to "confront and eradicate racism" in the world.

Thus, the authors argue for the importance of increasing educational leaders' racial awareness. The idea is that as leaders come to know more and understand the work of racial justice, they will act and behave more equitably. Moreover, the authors explicitly provide anti-racist tools to support practitioners in their work in navigating policies that can make a real difference for young people. Conceptually, the book draws from "color-evasiveness" as a tool to describe how too many leaders approach and advance their work. Complicating traditional notions of colorblindness, Diem and Welton describe how school leaders move away from color-evasiveness to race-consciousness for the sake of the communities in which they serve. Indeed, while illuminating the ways market-driven policies have been detrimental to advancing anti-racist agendas, this book works to "dismantle the racist ideologies, structures, and processes" that maintain discrimination and the status quo.

I strongly endorse this book as it will have wide appeal for the scholarly community – researchers, theorists, and policy makers – as well as educators in schools across the United States.

H. Richard Milner IV,
Cornelius Vanderbilt Distinguished Professor of Education;
author of Start Where You Are, But Don't Stay There
(2nd Edition, Harvard Education Press, 2020)

REFERENCE

Wagoner, N. (2016). Colin Kaepernick takes knee for anthem; joined by teammate Eric Reid, *ESPN*, September 2. Retrieved from www.espn.com/nfl/story/_/id/17444691/colin-kaepernick-san-francisco-49ers-sits-again-national-anthem.

Preface

While no one would ever deem the role of an educational leader as easy, it is particularly challenging in our current times. It seems like every day we wake up to a news story about another horrific racial incident that occurred in a school or community. And while hate and racism have always been a part of American culture, in recent years we have seen a spreading of hate in the United States and around the world, which is often linked to white supremacist and nationalist ideologies, and how it manifests itself into unspeakable atrocities such as school shootings, racial incidents in schools and on college campuses, and racial threats directed toward educators and students. Educational leaders play a critical role in identifying this hate and preventing it from crossing the doors of their schools. They must also understand their roles as policy actors and what they can do to push back at an educational system that was not created to provide opportunity for all students.

For years we have discussed and been frustrated with our field often thinking about educational leadership as one thing and educational policy as a completely separate entity. We find this to be a dangerous proposition as educational leaders' everyday practices are directly impacted by policy at the local, state, and national levels. Further, policy contexts today largely ignore the role of racism in education and how market-driven policies exacerbate racial inequality. How can we expect our schools to be anti-racist sites if as educators we fail to understand how racism is intertwined with policy, which directly impacts how our schools operate on a daily basis?

We chose to embark on this book journey so that we could in some way assist educational leaders in better comprehending the racial implications and challenges of the current educational policy landscape. As professors in departments of educational leadership and policy studies, we find ourselves cobbling together different articles and book chapters to share with our students that speak to anti-racist leadership and educational policy but have yet to find one comprehensive text that brings all of these ideas together. We hope that our book will be that one text that serves as a useful resource for courses in educational leadership programs that prepare future teacher leaders, principals, and superintendents. Our book speaks directly to how market-based policies that are color-evasive ignore the role of race and racism in education, and how these policies once implemented can negatively affect educational administrators' roles as leaders and implicate them in reproducing racism in their districts and schools.

Our book begins with an overview of how market-based and color-evasive ideological and political strategies go hand-in-hand and have unfortunately become a normal part of educational leadership practice. Also, the current sociopolitical context exacerbates a color-evasive, market-oriented state that has been in place in the U.S. for the last several decades. We discuss the importance of educational leaders moving away from policy discussions that use competition and capitalist strategies to address the problems faced by chronically underperforming schools because while these policy solutions appear to resolve inequality in education, they instead preserve white political interests. In Chapters 2–7, we examine prominent educational policy issues—demographic change, school choice, school closure, standardized testing and data use, school funding, and school discipline—unpacking how the policy rhetoric and agendas encompassing these issues are color-evasive and market-driven, and thus perpetuate racism in public education. We chose to focus on these specific policy issues as they are some of the more prevalent issues educational leaders across different sociopolitical and geographical contexts are facing on a daily basis. They are also issues being debated at local, state, and federal levels and covered regularly in media outlets. At the conclusion of each chapter, and what we believe is a distinctive feature of our book, we provide discussion questions about the policy issues that will ideally incite critical conversations among educational leaders and their school communities, as well as recommended readings and resources to help continue the conversation and knowledge-building around the policies and practices.

While Chapters 2–7 help readers become more racially aware of how color-evasive, market-driven educational policies and practices operate in school systems, we wanted to conclude the book with some type of tool that would assist educators in planning for and taking action to avoid the racial inequities these policies may cause when implemented. In the final chapter of the book, we propose an anti-racist policy decision-making protocol educational leaders can use to inform their practices when they confront color-evasive, market-driven policies. The decision-making protocol we present draws on a number of socially just policy models and equity audit processes from scholars who have come before us, and so we hope our tool can add to the canon of pedagogical apparatuses that connect research, theory, and practice. However, the contribution we try to make in our six-phase protocol is placing race front and center, exposing the systemic racism that is a result of color-evasive, market-driven educational policies.

Acknowledgments

This book would not have been possible without the many people in our lives who have been constant supporters of our work and well-being. Special thanks, most importantly, to Michelle D. Young, Mark Gooden, Gerardo López and Rich Milner for the mentorship each of you have provided to us over the years as graduate students and now colleagues, and for endorsing our book; many thanks also to Rich Milner for providing its foreword. To The University of Texas at Austin family, we are grateful for our time on the third floor of the George I. Sánchez Building as graduate students and being in a space that cultivated critical thinking. We are also appreciative of the many scholars who have come before us and continue to push our thinking and inform our work every day. The list is too great to include everyone we are indebted to but we would like to give thanks to James D. Anderson, Jeffrey S. Brooks, Casey Cobb, Jennifer Jellison Holme, Cris Mayo, Richard Reddick, Jay D. Scribner, Linda Tillman, and Eboni Zamani-Gallaher.

During the course of writing this book we were both granted semester-long sabbaticals so that we could focus our efforts on making this contribution a reality. We would like to thank the University of Missouri and University of Illinois at Urbana-Champaign, and particularly our individual departments and colleagues, for their encouragement and commitment to us as scholars pursuing our academic endeavors. We would also like to thank the graduate students in both of our departments for being willing to be challenged, and for challenging us, to imagine what anti-racist leadership can and should look like in our schools and beyond. Our students push us to be better professors and individuals and we hope the work reflected in this book makes you proud of us.

Thank you to Heather Jarrow, our publisher at Routledge, for your patience and unwavering support of our project. From the minute we proposed our idea to you at the American Educational Research Association Annual Meeting in San Antonio, Texas, to providing us more time to complete our work so we could be present for other commitments in our lives, we are so grateful and appreciate you.

Finally, we both want to thank our families for their love and being our first teachers of justice.

Chapter 1

Anti-Racism and Color-Evasiveness in a Neoliberal Context
An Introduction

In May 2019, the Southern Poverty Law Center (SPLC), a nonpartisan civil rights organization that has been operating for almost 50 years and is dedicated to fighting hate, seeking justice, and teaching tolerance, released a special report entitled *Hate at School*, which documents the rise of racism, xenophobia, anti-Semitism, and other forms of bigotry occurring in schools across the United States. Specifically, the report notes that while the SPLC identified 821 hate-related incidents in schools that were reported in the media in all of 2018, the nearly 2,800 educators who participated in the SPLC's survey stated that over 3,000 of these types of incidents occurred in just the fall of 2018. Further, most of the incidents were driven by racism *and* were not addressed by school leaders (Costello & Dillard, 2019).

These figures should be alarming to all of us. However, given what is currently happening in the larger U.S. sociopolitical context, sadly, we should not be surprised when we hear about the latest incident in which white male students are proudly giving the Nazi salute or when a Latinx student is told that she does not belong in the country and should "go home." Indeed, schools are not impervious to what is occurring every day in the larger society. Yet, they can be critical sites where such issues are addressed, making it increasingly important that we work to better equip those leading our schools with the tools necessary to confront such acts of hate and racism as well as the racial disparities that continue to pervade our public schools.

Racial inequities in educational opportunities largely continue to exist because district and school communities often try to address these inequities through technical fixes that are color-evasive and largely ignore the role that institutional and structural racism play in creating these gaps in opportunity (Castagno, 2014; Milner, 2012; Welton, Diem, & Holme, 2015). Unfortunately, these catchall solutions to racial differences in student achievement end up blaming students from low-income families and students of color for school failure, rather than the system charged with serving them (Ladson-Billings, 2006; Leonardo, 2007; Milner, 2012). Moreover, even when educational leaders do attempt to ideologically promote racial equity and diversity, they face faculty, staff, and community members who push back and even resist these efforts to shift norms and values. As a result, if educational leaders capitulate to any resistance to supporting racial equity, district and school level deficit attitudes and mindsets about students of color and their families will most likely go relatively unaddressed and the racial status quo may remain unchanged (Castagno, 2014; Lewis & Diamond, 2015; Welton et al., 2015).

Ultimately, what has been found in the research on districts and schools that engage in strategic improvement processes to achieve racial equity is that their good intentions often never really lead to full systemic and ongoing action to redress the inequities that exist (Castagno, 2014; Lewis & Diamond, 2015; Welton et al., 2015). Consequently, we need anti-racist educational leaders who are trained and prepared to face the political complexity and uncertainty that will undoubtedly occur when they advance racial equity in their district and school communities. It is only when educational leaders establish a common language for why discussing issues of race is indeed important, and model how to do so, that the rest of the district and/or school community will feel they have the space, buy-in, and sense of urgency to do the same. Thus, to actively be anti-racist in both their values and practices, educational leaders need to understand the system of racism, its influence on society, and purposefully act to confront issues pertaining to race and racism in their districts and school communities (Brooks, 2012; Diem & Carpenter, 2013; Gooden & Dantley, 2012; Gooden & O'Doherty, 2015; Young & Laible, 2000).

Educational leaders are responsible for articulating to their staff why racial equity is important and also lead their staff in the district/school improvement planning processes that are critical to achieving racial equity. This is particularly important as research shows that a school's academic performance and achievement is largely determined by the quality and effectiveness of the school administration's leadership, especially their leadership in supporting teachers' instruction and fostering a positive school-wide culture (Kellough & Hill, 2015; Wallace Foundation, 2013). Ultimately, expanding research on anti-racist leadership will give educational leaders the practical tools needed to guide their district/school communities through change processes that are important to racial equity work.

ANTI-RACISM AND ANTI-RACIST LEADERSHIP

Anti-racism is defined as the system of thoughts and practices that aim to confront and eradicate racism as well as ideologies and practices that promote equality for racial and ethnic groups (Blakeney, 2005; Bonnett, 2000). Everyday anti-racism considers how individuals work towards combatting racism in their daily lives, practice, and/or lived contexts (Aquino, 2016; Pollock, 2008). In the field of education, research on anti-racism examines the pedagogical tools, or anti-racist pedagogy, useful to teaching about anti-racism or how to actively be anti-racist in practice (Kishimoto, 2018; Pollock, 2008). However, most of the research on anti-racism in education is in teacher education, focusing on how either pre-service teachers become racially aware or how teachers use anti-racist pedagogy in their classroom teaching (de Freitas & McAuley, 2008; Milner, 2010; Mosley, 2010; Ohito, 2016; Raby, 2004; Ulluci, 2011; Welton, Harris, La Londe, & Moyer, 2015). Furthermore, the limited research on anti-racist leadership that does exist tends to focus on three main areas: problem identification, recognizing that leaders need better preparation, and professional development on how to be anti-racist leaders; however, the research falls short in offering specific strategies for *how* to engage in these efforts.

While we are certainly not dismissing the importance of the research that does exist on anti-racist teacher education and leadership, much of which includes examining color-evasive mentalities, pushing back against the existence of a meritocracy, the perpetuation of deficit thinking, the lack of culturally responsive curricula and reflexive thinking about race in the classroom, as well as tackling the (often non-existent) discussion on whiteness and its role in education and the larger society (Brooks, Arnold, & Brooks, 2013; Carpenter & Diem, 2013; Gooden & Dantley, 2012; Gooden & O'Doherty, 2015; Milner, 2010; Milner & Howard, 2013; Pollock, 2010; Sleeter, 2014), we think more research needs to focus on how leaders "ensure their everyday actions are drawn from an antiracist orientation" and what practices they need to engage in that purposively address "social, political, and educational oppression" (Diem, Carpenter, & Lewis-Durham, 2019, p. 711).

We are living in a sociopolitical climate where we constantly hear the rhetoric around paying attention to and being respective of "both sides" of an issue. While we agree that there are often differing opinions around hot button issues, when it comes to racism, there are not "good people on both sides" of the discussion. Racism and white supremacy, as Burkholder (2018) notes, are "inherently wrong and tremendously dangerous to American democracy" (n.p.). Further, while school leaders operate in a context that is increasingly political, being an anti-racist school leader is fundamentally a political act. Indeed, school leaders are called to advocate for the needs of their school communities and address equity and cultural responsiveness in their leadership practices, as outlined in the Professional Standards for Educational Leaders (NPBEA, 2015). Thus, with this book we aim to demonstrate that central to such practices is addressing racism and ensuring that schools, and those who operate within them, are aware of how racism manifests itself in policies that ultimately dictate practice.

WHITENESS AND WHITE FRAGILITY

Part of the work associated with anti-racist leadership is recognizing the factors that work every day to undermine anti-racism, factors such as whiteness, white fragility, and anti-Blackness. DiAngelo (2011) defines whiteness as

> the specific dimensions of racism that serve to elevate White people over people of color...Whiteness is dynamic, relational, and operating at all times and on myriad levels. These processes and practices include basic rights, values, beliefs, perspectives and experiences purported to be commonly shared by all but which are actually only consistently afforded to White people.
>
> (p. 56)

Whiteness has value and therefore a possessive investment in it, which compels white Americans, in particular, to "invest" in an identity that rewards them with power, opportunity, and resources (Lipsitz, 1998). Whiteness has real ramifications for (in)opportunity in society, in large part through policies that have been (re)created to privilege white individuals. Whiteness also perpetuates anti-Blackness and a discourse that blames Black people and people of color for existent inequities rather than acknowledge the advantages from just being a white person in society (Lipsitz, 1998).

When white people are challenged by their racial privilege, they often become defensive, angry, fearful, and personalize racism. DiAngelo (2011) calls these acts and associated behaviors such as silence or argumentation "white fragility." Specifically, DiAngelo defines white fragility as "a state in which even a minimum amount of racial stress becomes intolerable" to white individuals causing them to become defensive, which then reifies "white racial equilibrium" (p. 57). White fragility is perpetuated by a number of factors, including white people living racially segregated lives; viewing themselves and their experiences as "universal" and representative of all "human experiences"; valuing individuals and individualism rather than seeing how white people are part of a racialized group just like other racial groups; desiring racial comfort, racial arrogance, racial belonging, being "free" from thinking about race; and the consistent messaging of "white superiority" (DiAngelo, 2011, pp. 58–63). The very existence of white fragility demonstrates the possessive investment of whiteness and why the failure to disinvest in it prevents us from genuinely addressing racism.

ANTI-BLACKNESS

The schooling experience of Black students in the U.S. continues to be one of dehumanization. Indeed, there are countless examples of anti-Blackness and violence against Black bodies in schools, from the lack of opportunity and access to quality education, to body shaming and banning hairstyles such as locs or afros; violent disciplinary actions; reinforcing stereotypes; and making outright racial slurs as if they were part of the acceptable school vernacular. Dumas (2016) argues "that any incisive analyses of racial(ized) discourse and policy process in education must grapple with cultural disregard for and disgust with blackness" and examines "how a theorization of antiblackness allows one to more precisely identify and respond to racism in education discourse and in the formation and implementation of education policy" (p. 12). We agree with Dumas and believe that being an anti-racist school leader includes being cognizant of how the education system is centered around anti-Blackness (Dancy, Edwards, & Davis, 2018), an understanding of which in turn can lead to designing and implementing more implicit anti-racist school policies and practices.

Dumas and ross (2016) note that "antiblackness is not simply racism against Black people" but instead "refers to a broader antagonistic relationship between blackness and (the possibility of) humanity" (p. 429). Dancy et al. (2018) add, "White humanity is dependent on its ability to harm Black life. To avoid violence against Black people would place White humanity in question because, in an anti-Black polity, White humanity is predicated on Black inhumanity" (p. 188). Acknowledging anti-Blackness is therefore different than simply stating that racism and white privilege exist and are problematic; anti-Blackness is comprehending the Black condition and how the dehumanization of Black people has resulted in historical and contemporary acts of violence toward Black bodies (Dumas, 2016).

Anti-Black deficit practices and policies in education are certainly not new and are in fact pervasive in marginalizing Black students, particularly when it comes to academic outcomes. However, school leaders are in powerful positions to contest anti-Blackness and provide meaningful opportunities with their school communities to discuss the ramifications of anti-Blackness. It is only when these critical discussions occur that we can begin to envision an education system that values Black students.

COLOR-EVASIVENESS

School leaders often find the revolving door of school policies and reforms they are tasked with implementing as the one arena that seems to be outside of their locus of control (Rallis, Rossman, Reagan, Cobb, & Kuntz, 2008). This is particularly the case when educational policies come from the top down as educational leaders typically have little input on how such policies may affect their school and district communities. Educational leaders also have limited time to consider the potential racial implications of policies, thus pushing them to [color-]evasively implement policy (Diem, Welton, Frankenberg, & Holme, 2016; Holme, Diem, & Welton, 2014; Welton et al., 2015). This level of racial unawareness amongst school and/or district leadership is indeed problematic because when leaders indiscriminately implement policies that overlook and in many ways discount how institutional racism is at the root of the problem, they unintentionally exacerbate any racial inequities that may already exist (Diem et al., 2016; Frankenberg, 1993; Ryan, 2012).

Much of educational leaders' anxiety about the limited control they have over the policy process as it relates to race, equity, and opportunity stems from the current educational landscape where educational policies are not only *color-evasive* but also *market-driven*. *Color-evasive* policies maintain the racial status quo through the adoption of race-neutral policies that *deny* the role race and racism play in perpetuating structural inequities (Bonilla-Silva, 2017; Leonardo, 2007). Ruth Frankenberg introduced the concept *color-evasiveness* in her 1993 book *White Women, Race Matters: The Social Construction of Whiteness*. Frankenberg defines color-evasiveness as an "act of dodging difference" or to disregard racial differences that exist in society (p. 142). Therefore, those who adopt a color-evasive mindset argue that racism is no longer an issue, and what racial inequities do exist are the fault of people of color because in society today they have the same opportunities as white people (Frankenberg, 1993). This "evasiveness" towards racial differences also then leads to a dismissiveness and "complicity" towards institutional and structural forms of racism and racial inequality (Frankenberg, 1993). Also, color-evasiveness is a white supremacy strategy that any of us (both white and people of color) can be at fault of or implicated in enacting.

Yet, complicity, dismissiveness, denial, and ignoring the permanence of racism in society is just one way in which color-evasiveness plays out in policy and practice. Color-evasiveness can even be a tool for those who do acknowledge that racial differences exist, however, they address race in "safer" and more "polite" terms (Frankenberg, 1993, pp. 142, 149). Thus, the recognition of racial differences is "selective" only to the celebration of cultural differences commonly practiced in cultural diversity and multiculturalism discourses, and fails to be critical of the historical power differences that still remain between white people and people of color. Still, typically those who engage in less "dangerous" approaches to addressing race minimally make a good faith effort to look into the racial inequities that exist, but do so in a relatively uncritical way that by design keeps the racial power hierarchy/status quo intact (Frankenberg, 1993, p. 142; also see Gorski, 2019; Swanson & Welton, 2019).

Evading race may seem like the less *dangerous* approach at addressing racism, but this approach has long-term consequences. Ultimately, society's collective evasiveness toward racism only further *endangers* people of color, who must continue to endure the long-term effects of racism ignored and left unresolved. Because these *dangerous* and *evasive* approaches to race have now become commonsense to our society, it is ever more important that policy makers and educational leaders are trained to be critical and even suspicious of color-evasive education policies and practices that are simplistic, passive and avoid the "tension" and "struggle" needed to tackle racial injustices in education (Leonardo & Porter, 2010, p. 144; Swanson & Welton, 2019). Even though the needle towards achieving racial justice continues to move forward, it moves at a very slow pace because we as a society remain color-evasive and still tiptoe around openly calling out the racism and racist structures that exist in society at-large and in education specifically. Hence, we need policy makers and educational leaders who are not just conscious of how racism plays out in "historical, political, social, or cultural terms rather than essentialist ones" but are also anti-racist in their actions to redress and eliminate racist attitudes, policies, structures, and practices (Frankenberg, 1993, p. 157).

Challenging the Term Colorblindness

Now that we have presented how we are conceptualizing and critiquing color-evasive policies and practices in this book, you, the reader, are probably thinking, "Instead of color-evasiveness, don't you really mean colorblindness?". Yes, in our past work we have used the term colorblindness to describe educational policies and practices that pretend race is not an issue but in reality are racist. For instance, we used the term colorblindness in our research to describe school district leaders' responses to how their communities are increasingly racially diversifying (Diem et al., 2016; Welton et al., 2015), as well as the race-neutral approaches white principals used when addressing issues of race with their staff (Swanson & Welton, 2019). We even critiqued how former President Obama's My Brother's Keeper (MBK) Initiative largely burdened young men of color with saving themselves from their own racial oppression and did little in terms of addressing how institutional racism is in fact the root cause (Welton & Diem, 2016).

However, after reading an article by Annamma, Jackson, and Morrison (2017) we were pushed to question how using the word *colorblindness* to describe the act of not *seeing* the prevalence of race and racism in society may result in a deficit conception of people with dis/abilities, especially a person who is blind, or a person with a visual impairment or low vision. According to Annamma et al. the word *colorblindness*,

> As a racial ideology, conflates lack of eyesight with lack of knowing. Said differently, the inherent ableism in this term equates blindness with ignorance. However, inability to see is not ignorance; in fact, blindness

provides unique ways of understanding the world to which sighted people have no access.

(p. 154)

Moreover, the authors critique how scholars of race often forget that, like race, dis/ability is also a social construction. So, the use of the word colorblindness is a simultaneous social construction of race and ability that unfortunately socializes us to view dis/ability as a deficit (Annamma et al., 2017). To take account of this, instead of colorblindness, Annamma et al. suggest using Ruth Frankenberg's (1993) concept of color-evasiveness. We will continue to challenge how we have conceptualized colorblindness in our own work—both prior and future—and are taking this opportunity to model how scholars and practitioners should always take stock and reflect on how discourse impacts research and practice and how it is continuously evolving. Thus, from this point forward we are using color-evasiveness to describe the deliberate avoidance of discussions about race and racism and the outright denial that the structural and everyday racism people of color face exists in society today (Annamma et al., 2017).

EDUCATIONAL POLICY AND POLITICS

Public policy is a complex and "value-laden" process in which political systems aim to address a specific societal problem (Fowler, 2013, p. 5). Conflict in policymaking is important to shake up the status quo and achieve change, and conflict is also inevitable in a democratic process where multiple perspectives and ideas come to the fore. Therefore, in policymaking democratic deliberation is essential for all voices to come together, dialogue, and achieve a common understanding on how the policy goals and subsequent policy actions can serve the public good. So, policymaking should happen *in* the community and *with* the community (Fowler, 2013).

Yet, the word *public* when attached to *policy* assumes that the process of identifying problems and then strategizing how to use policy to address these problems is democratic, deliberative, and truly *public* (see Rallis et al., 2008). Unfortunately, public policy has never been a just, open process intended to serve the public good. Instead *public* policy is a constant battle amongst *private* interests where those who have the power and privilege to do so ensure their interests prevail, particularly when policy is designed with equitable intentions to right racial wrongs. This is especially so in our current policy environment where business leaders, the media, and politicians all believe that public education is in a state of crisis, and therefore now all have an opinion on how to fix public education (Fowler, 2013). A central pattern throughout the history of U.S. public policy is that dominant groups are resolutely threatened when policies are designed to serve the needs and level the playing field for minoritized groups. Dominant groups are thus typically only willing to endorse an equity-driven policy when the policy serves their interests as well. The 1954 *Brown v. Board of Education* decision declared separate but equal schools unconstitutional, however, at the time white Americans were only willing to recognize the harmful effects of racial segregation when at the height of the Cold War the United States' reputation as a superpower was at stake for its unequal treatment of Black people (Bell, 1980). The *Brown* decision is a prime example of *interest convergence* where any policy change that intends to achieve racial equity only occurs when it aligns with the interests of white stakeholders (Bell, 1980).

The power imbalances—that is, white supremacy—that play out in the policy process in order to preserve white interests are the reason why a traditional approach to policymaking is insufficient to redress racial injustice. A traditional policy approach assumes that policymaking can be planned, managed, and transpires in the following stages: issue definition, agenda setting, policy formulation, policy adoption, and implementation (Diem, Young, Welton, Mansfield, & Lee, 2014). Consequently, in our analysis of each policy issue highlighted in this book we also couple anti-racism with critical approaches to policy analysis (see Diem et al., 2014). A critical approach to policy analysis tracks the policy process to uncover any discrepancies between the policy rhetoric and reality, the intended versus the unintended consequences of policy, how the policy unfolds from its development to actual implementation, and how we are then socialized and normed by the policy rhetoric (Diem et al., 2014). Finally, critical approaches to policy analysis expose how a particular policy perpetuates imbalances in power, resources, and knowledge (Diem et al., 2014); in this book we therefore use critical approaches to policy analysis to speak truth to the racism that exists in educational policy and politics.

The Racialization of Market-Driven Educational Policies

Market-driven policies operate under the ideology of neoliberalism, which has been heavily critiqued as it goes against what is important to achieving racial equity in order to prioritize individualism, self-interest, reduction in labor costs, marketization, deregulation, privatization, and consumerism over policy initiatives that would instead create equitable opportunities for *all* students. Lipman (2011) defines neoliberalism as "an ensemble of economic and social policies, forms of governance, and discourses and ideologies that promote individual self-interest, unrestricted flows of capital, deep reductions in the cost of labor and sharp retrenchment of the public sphere" (p. 6). Moreover, "Neoliberalism is an ideological project to reconstruct values, social relations, and social identities—to produce a new social imagery" (Lipman, 2011, p. 10). Au and Ferrare (2015) build upon Lipman's conceptualization of neoliberalism, defining it as

> a massive restructuring structure, one that restructures commonsense, restructures relationships between humans and other humans, restructures relationships between humans and products, restructures cultural, capital, political flows, and restructures the state and economy in line with individual self-interest and at a cost to commitments to collective well-being.
>
> (p. 3)

This restructuring of our society that Lipman (2011) and Au and Ferrare (2015) discuss is a move from valuing the collective to promoting the individual. This restructuring also pushes us further away from valuing public goods in favor of private goods, which then results in a system where people are constantly competing with each other for goods in the marketplace, ultimately resulting in winners and losers. Under this neoliberal ideology, since we as individuals are responsible for ourselves and our ability to succeed, we are also responsible for our failures and it is therefore our fault if we are unable to succeed in the free marketplace (Lipman, 2015).

In its attempt to restructure how we think and what we should value, neoliberalism is also quick to deny the role of race in market-driven policies. Neoliberals are color-evasive and claim that inequalities that continue to exist are not related to race since we are decades past the Civil Rights Era and policies have been enacted to provide equal opportunity for all. Operating from this color-evasive mindset denies how structures and policies implemented years prior to and post the Civil Rights Era continue to reverberate in society, resulting in continued, and what some argue is "intensified structural inequality based on race" (Lipman, 2011, p. 13). While neoliberals attempt to conceal race in their reform efforts, it is undeniable that white supremacy and white dominance is maintained in larger part through the expansion of neoliberalism (Lipman, 2015; Picower & Mayorga, 2015). Indeed, in the United States, neoliberalism is deeply intertwined with race.

In education, neoliberalism seeks to apply business principles to school reform. Moreover, the market-driven policies and practices currently implemented in education are color-evasive as they use capitalist strategies like privatization that pretend to be race-neutral but in reality, have significant racial implications that preserve the racial status quo (Picower & Mayorga, 2015). Market-driven educational policies like school choice, school closure, and high-stakes accountability (which we will discuss in further detail in this book) are particularly prevalent in urban school districts where they are worsening already deep divisions existent in cities (Scott & Holme, 2016), "reconfigure key aspects of [public] education policy and practice", and usurp the purpose of public education (Au & Ferrare, 2015, pp. 5–8). By allowing entrepreneurs and corporations to dictate and ultimately profit from the education system, what becomes of value in public schools is more aligned to what is valued in the private sector (Au & Ferrare, 2015). Further, these "market-based reforms can perpetuate and reify social, policy, and economic inequality unless strong regulations allow for more equitable implementation" (Scott & Holme, 2016, p. 282), but for strong regulations we first require the existence of racially-conscious educational leaders. Also, with a current U.S. Secretary of Education who has a track record of supporting market-driven policies and practices such as the privatization of education and local control, nationally there is a level of uncertainty of educational policies on the horizon, and how this impending neoliberal ideology will impact a school leader who advocates for equity, especially when it comes to racial matters (Strauss, 2016).

Neoliberal reform efforts in education are not new. Starting in the 1980s after the publication of *A Nation at Risk* (U.S. NCEE, 1983) and the perceived lack of quality education offered in our public schools, which led to an era of standardization and high-stakes testing via the passage of the No Child Left Behind Act of 2001, followed by Race to the Top (2009) and the expansion of charter schools, and now the current Every Students Succeeds Act (2015) era, neoliberalism has taken hold of the educational policy discourse, which directly impacts leadership because administrators are the ones responsible for carrying out policies. Market-driven policies become problematic for school leaders because these policies encourage catchall solutions that do not consider the contextual differences and needs across educational settings, which as a result ignores the racial inequities already inherent within the system (see Milner, 2010, 2012). Instead, we need a radical restructuring of the educational system to eventually level the playing field. We also need more educational scholars to focus on both the neoliberal turn in education and how race plays a role in these efforts. In our book, we discuss how school administrators can reconcile the ethical dilemmas they face in a market-driven educational policy context that pushes them to be color-evasive in their leadership practice.

WHY THIS BOOK?

Educational policymaking today is dominated by *market-driven* policies that are largely designed to be *color-evasive*, ignoring the reality of racism in education. Therefore, one objective of this book is to discuss how this color-evasive and market-driven policy context affects school administrators' leadership practices. This book centers its attention on school leaders because they are the ones who are ultimately on the front line helping their school community make sense of the policies they are confronted with implementing. Our book aims to equip school leaders with the tools to question whether a policy explicitly addresses racism in schooling or fails to do so because it is inherently color-evasive. We provide examples of how leaders can encourage their school community to respond in a manner that instead promotes racial equity.

We chose the title *Anti-Racist Educational Leadership and Policy: Addressing Racism in Public Education* because educational leaders should not overlook the current color-evasive, market-oriented educational policy agenda that is largely responsible for the racial inequities that exist in schools today. Indeed, for decades policies at the federal, state, and local levels were created to lead people to believe that justice is racially neutral, but those individuals who created these policies are in fact fully aware of their racial implications (Rothstein, 2017). Instead, educational leaders should be cognizant of the realities of racial injustice in education and have a willingness to truly acknowledge how these policies can negatively impact how they lead. Furthermore, our book helps educational leaders understand how policies that are both color-evasive and market-driven in design are a form of neoliberalism that can potentially unravel any efforts they make as leaders alongside their school and/or district community to achieve racial equity. We emphasize how important it is for educational leaders to use an anti-racist lens to not only anticipate but also counter color-evasive, market-driven policies, and provide strategies for how to do so. Therefore, the contributions to the field this book aims to accomplish are as follows:

1. **Increase educational leaders' racial awareness**. Educational leaders must first expand their foundational awareness of how racism in education transpires before they can fully learn how to critically examine educational policies that are conceivably color-evasive and market-driven. Hence, we first review concepts key to the historical, institutional, structural, and political underpinnings of racism in education.
2. **Demystify the influence of the current color-evasive, market-driven educational policy context**. Most of the policies educational leaders encounter in today's educational policy context are market-based and by default will unfortunately pressure them to be color-evasive in their leadership practices. Therefore, throughout the book we focus on high-profile educational policy issues as case studies to discuss how each issue's color-evasive and market-driven agenda, if implemented without question, can compromise much of the work educational leaders do to advance racial equity.
3. **Provide anti-racist tools for navigating the policy process**. We conclude the book by offering a protocol for anti-racist policy decision-making that both educational leaders and policymakers can use to inform their practices, especially when confronting color-evasive, market-driven policies.

OVERVIEW OF THE BOOK

Each chapter of the book focuses on a single high-profile educational policy issue, analyzing it through a color-evasive, market-driven lens. Following the policy analysis in each chapter, we provide specific examples of ways in which school leaders can instead develop action-oriented solutions that are race-conscious; discussion questions to provoke dialogue among students and their faculty/staff; and additional resources (readings, websites, etc.) for further insight into the particular policy or practice. We conclude the book by presenting a protocol for anti-racist decision-making that educational leaders can use to inform their practices when they must confront color-evasive, market-driven policies. Ultimately, by discussing color-evasive and market-driven education policies in tandem, our book offers a new and important tool for leaders to guide their school communities through change processes that are vital to racial equity work.

In Chapter 1, "Anti-Racism and Color-Evasiveness in a Neoliberal Context: An Introduction," we have discussed the focus and purpose of the book and defined key concepts and ideas—anti-racism, color-evasiveness, and the racialization of market-driven policies—that will be explored further in subsequent chapters, each featuring a highly debated educational policy issue. For Chapter 2, "How School Leaders Respond to Demographic Change," we review literature on how school districts in various contexts respond to demographic change. We also examine the policies and practices school leaders design to racially diversify their schools, despite the federal government's continued reneging on policies like desegregation that seek to diversify district and school settings. We then consider how the market-oriented educational context may push educational leaders to respond to the growing racial diversity in their districts and schools in ways that are color-evasive. We conclude this chapter with examples of anti-racist approaches to promoting racially diverse schooling environments.

Next, in Chapter 3, "School Choice and Who Has a Right to Choose," we discuss the role of race in school choice and how a policy that was originally intended to promote racial integration by providing multiple schooling options from which students and families can choose has instead created a racially and socioeconomically unequal marketplace. It is assumed that the competition created from opening up the marketplace beyond traditional public school options to charter schools, vouchers, and open-enrollment programs will lead to the creation of higher quality and more efficient schools. However, we demonstrate how low-income and students and families of color do not necessarily have a choice within this free marketplace and unfortunately still end up in the lowest performing and least-resourced schools. We conclude with examples of ways in which districts are implementing school choice policies from a racial equity framework that ensures quality schooling is provided to *all* students no matter their race, socioeconomic status, or zip code.

Students, families, and community members of color are often left out of the decision-making process when their neighborhood school is slated to be closed. In Chapter 4, "The Racial Politics of School Closure and Community Response," we provide examples of ways in which local school parents and community activists across the country are organizing to keep their schools open, and what district and school administrators can learn from communities of color's fight for racial justice for their neighborhood schools. It is assumed that closing a school will give its students opportunities to transfer to higher quality schooling options, but we present research that suggests the opposite happens as it is Black and Latinx students and families who bear the burden of the negative effects that come with school closure. Following our analysis of school closure, we provide recommendations for how educational leadership should be envisioned as a collective effort among administrators, parents, teachers, and students working to put an end to disproportionately closing schools in Black and Latinx communities.

In Chapter 5, "Standardized Testing and the Racial Implications of Data Use," we critically examine the most recent iteration of the Elementary Secondary Education Act (ESEA), the Every Student Succeeds Act (ESSA). Although ESSA claims to emphasize equity more so than its predecessor, No Child Left Behind (NCLB), we demonstrate how the execution of equity under ESSA is still color-evasive, market-driven, and in some ways not a departure from the test-driven accountability system designed under NCLB. What differentiates ESSA from its predecessor is that the policy gives states the flexibility to design standards and assessments tailored to their students' needs. We give recommendations for how state and district level leaders can use the flexibility that ESSA provides to implement more anti-racist approaches to data-driven decision-making to improve student learning opportunities and outcomes. Then, in Chapter 6, "School Funding and the Need for Resource Redistribution," we examine the relationship of race and school funding by exploring how school finance has been litigated over time in the U.S. and how this has impacted current school funding policies and structures. Since the Great Recession of 2008, educational leaders feel immensely constrained when making decisions about how to best distribute funds and resources to their districts and schools. Most states use school funding systems that rely heavily on local property taxes to fund education that benefits property-wealthy districts, resulting in growing economic inequality between schools and districts in the U.S. that also coincides with existing racial disparities. After our analysis of school funding policies, we provide examples of how educational leaders can design more race-conscious solutions that dare to redistribute and restructure funding and resources to redress existing racial inequities.

In Chapter 7, "Racism and School Discipline: From Schools to Prison, or Schools *As* a Prison," we discuss the racial implications of exclusionary discipline practices and look at two specific education policy issues: zero tolerance policies and the role of policing and the criminalization of students of color in schools. Students of color, and Black students in particular, are not only disciplined at much higher rates than their peers but the discipline is more frequent and severe. These disciplinary actions place students on a path that significantly alters their academic and life trajectories and perpetuates what we know as the school-to-prison pipeline. In this chapter we look at how strategies such as Response to Intervention (RTI) and Positive Behavior Intervention Supports (PBIS) seek to offer better alternatives to exclusionary discipline practices but in reality often uphold what student behavior "should" look like, which is centered around white norms. We conclude the chapter by offering recommendations for more anti-racist discipline practices.

Finally, in our concluding Chapter 8, "A Protocol for Anti-Racist Policy Decision-Making in Educational Leadership," we propose an anti-racist policy decision-making protocol educational leaders can use to inform their practices when they confront color-evasive, market-driven policies. In Chapters 1 through 7 we help readers become more racially aware of how a number of color-evasive, market-driven educational policies and practices operate in school systems. Still, we want readers to use their newfound race-consciousness to then take action to avert the potential inequities these policies cause when implemented. To engage in more race-conscious processes, school leaders must lead their staff in developing a vision and common language for what it means to achieve racial equity in school policy, improvement, and practice (Welton et al., 2015), and so we see the protocol we developed as a tool that school leaders can use to accomplish this goal. Our protocol is similar to an equity audit process (Frattura & Capper, 2007; View et al., 2016) where educators work in teams to engage in a cycle of inquiry that involves examining where inequities exist within their district and/or schools and why. However, our decision-making tool helps leaders place *race* front and center. We also draw from a number of policy analysis models that provide educational leaders with strategies for policy implementation that are equitable and just (Kyser, Skelton, Warren, & Whiteman, 2016; Macey, Thorius, & Skelton, 2012; Rallis et al., 2008), discussing how these tools inform our anti-racist decision-making protocol.

Note: We follow the lead of scholars such as Matias, Viesca, Garrison-Wade, Tandon, & Galindo (2014) and Dumas (2016) and do not capitalize 'white' throughout the book as a way to challenge its oppressive nature. We only capitalize 'white' and 'whiteness' if they are presented as such in a direct quote. We capitalize Black throughout the book as we believe Black represents a racial identity group much like African American (and the two are often used synonymously) and as such deserves to be capitalized.

REFERENCES

Annamma, S. A., Jackson, D. D., & Morrison, D. (2017). Conceptualizing color-evasiveness: Using dis/ability critical race theory to expand a color-blind racial ideology in education and society. *Race Ethnicity and Education, 20*(2), 147–162.

Aquino, K. (2016). Anti-racism 'from below': Exploring repertoires of everyday anti-racism. *Ethnic and Racial Studies, 39*(1), 105–122.

Au, W., & Ferrare, J. J. (2015). Introduction: Neoliberalism, social networks, and the new governance of education. In W. Au & J. J. Ferrare (Eds.), *Mapping corporate education reform: Power and policy networks in a neoliberal state* (pp. 1–22). New York: Routledge.

Bell, D. (1980). *Brown v. Board of Education* and the interest-convergence dilemma. *Harvard Law Review, 93*(3), 518–533.

Blakeney, A. M. (2005). Antiracist pedagogy: Definition, theory, and professional development. *Journal of Curriculum and Pedagogy, 2*(1), 119–132.

Bonilla-Silva, E. (2017). *Racism without racists: Color-blind racism and the persistence of racial inequality in America* (5th edition). Lanham, MD: Rowman & Littlefield.

Bonnett, A. (2000). *Anti-racism.* New York: Routledge.

Brooks, J. S. (2012). *Black school, white school: Racism and educational (mis)leadership.* New York: Teachers College Press.

Brooks, J. S., Arnold, N. W., & Brooks, M. C. (2013). Educational leadership and racism: A narrative inquiry into second-generation segregation. *Teachers College Record, 115*(11), 1–27.

Burkholder, Z. (2018). Can we legislate anti-racist education? New Jersey says we can, Pittsburgh says we must. *Teachers College Record.*

Carpenter, B. W., & Diem, S. (2013). Talking race: Facilitating critical conversations in educational leadership preparation programs. *Journal of School Leadership, 23*(6), 902–931.

Castagno, A. E. (2014). *Educated in whiteness: Good intentions and diversity in schools.* Minneapolis, MN: University of Minnesota Press.

Costello, M., & Dillard, C. (2019). *Hate at school.* Montgomery, AL: Southern Poverty Law Center.

Dancy II, T. E., Edwards, K. T., & Davis, J. E. (2018). Historically white universities and plantation politics: Anti-blackness and higher education in the Black Lives Matter era. *Urban Education, 53*(2), 176–195.

de Freitas, E., & McAuley, A. (2008). Teaching for diversity by troubling whiteness: Strategies for classrooms in isolated white communities. *Race Ethnicity and Education, 11*(4), 429–444.

DiAngelo, R. (2011). White fragility. *International Journal of Critical Pedagogy, 3*(3), 54–70.

Diem, S., & Carpenter, B. W. (2013). Examining race-related silences: Interrogating the education of tomorrow's educational leaders. *Journal of Research in Leadership Education, 8*(1), 56–76.

Diem, S., Carpenter, B. W., & Lewis-Durham, T. (2019). Preparing antiracist school leaders in a school choice context. *Urban Education, 54*(5), 706–731.

Diem, S., Welton, A. D., Frankenberg, E., & Holme, J. J. (2016). Racial diversity in the suburbs: How race-neutral responses to demographic change perpetuate inequity in suburban school districts. *Race Ethnicity and Education, 19*(4), 731–762.

Diem, S., Young, M. D., Welton, A., Mansfield, K., & Lee, P. (2014). The intellectual landscape of critical policy analysis. *International Journal of Qualitative Studies in Education, 27*(9), 1068–1090.

Dumas, M. J. (2016). Against the dark: Antiblackness in education policy and discourse. *Theory Into Practice, 55*(1), 11–19.

Dumas, M. J., & ross, k. m. (2016). 'Be real Black for me': Imagining BlackCrit in education. *Urban Education, 51*(4), 415–442.

Every Child Succeeds Act (ESSA) of 2015, Public Law No. 114-95, S.1177, 114th Cong. (2015).

Fowler, F. C. (2013). *Policy studies for educational leaders: An introduction, 4th edition*. Boston, MA: Allyn & Bacon/Pearson

Frankenberg, R. (1993). *White women, race matters: The social construction of whiteness*. Minneapolis, MN: University of Minnesota Press.

Frattura, E. M., & Capper, C. A. (2007). *Leading for social justice: Transforming schools for all learners*. Thousand Oaks, CA: Corwin Press.

Gooden, M. A., & Dantley, M. (2012). Centering race in a framework for leadership preparation. *Journal of Research on Leadership in Education, 7*(2), 235–251.

Gooden, M. A., & O'Doherty, A. (2015). Do you see what I see? Fostering aspiring leaders' racial awareness. *Urban Education, 50*(2), 225–255.

Gorski, P. (2019). Avoiding racial equity detours. *Educational Leadership, 76*(7), 56–61.

Holme, J. J., Diem, S., & Welton, A.D. (2014). Suburban school districts and demographic change: The technical, normative, and political dimensions of response. *Educational Administration Quarterly, 50*(1), 34–66.

Kellough, R. D., & Hill, P. H. (2015). *Understanding the role of today's school principal: A primer for bridging theory to practice* (2nd ed.). Lanham, MD: Rowman & Littlefield.

Kishimoto, K. (2018). Anti-racist pedagogy: From faculty's self-reflection to organizing within and beyond the classroom. *Race Ethnicity and Education, 21*(4), 540–554.

Kyser, T. S., Skelton, S. M., Warren, C. L., & Whiteman, R. S. (2016). *Policy equity analysis toolkit*. Indianapolis, IN: Great Lakes Equity Center. Retrieved from http://glec.education.iupui.edu/Images/equity_tools/2016_03_25_Policy%20Toolkit_FINAL.pdf

Ladson-Billings, G. (2006). From the achievement gap to the education debt: Understanding achievement in U.S. schools. *Educational Researcher, 35*(7), 3–12.

Leonardo, Z. (2007). The war on schools: NCLB, nation creation and the educational construction of whiteness. *Race Ethnicity and Education, 10*(3), 261–278.

Leonardo, Z., & Porter, R. K. (2010). Pedagogy of fear: Toward a Fanonian theory of "safety" in race dialogue. *Race Ethnicity and Education, 13*(2), 139–157.

Lewis, A. E., & Diamond, J. B. (2015). *Despite the best intentions: How racial inequality thrives in good schools.* New York: Oxford University Press.

Lipman, P. (2011). *The new political economy of urban education: Neoliberalism, race, and the right to the city.* New York: Routledge.

Lipman, P. (2015). Capitalism, race, and the role of schools in social transformation: A response. *Educational Theory, 65*(3), 341–349.

Lipsitz, G. (1998). *The possessive investment in whiteness: How white people profit from identity politics.* Philadelphia, PA: Temple University Press.

Macey, E. M., Thorius, K. A. K., & Skelton, S. M. (2012). *Equity by design: Engaging school communities in critical reflection on policy.* Indianapolis, IN: Great Lakes Equity Center. Retrieved from http://glec.education.iupui.edu/assets/files/2013_5_1_PolicyBrief_FINAL.pdf

Matias, C. E., Viesca, K. M., Garrison-Wade, D. F., Tandon, M., & Galindo, R. (2014). "What is critical whiteness studies doing in OUR nice field like critical race theory?" Applying CRT and CWS to understand the white imaginations of white teacher candidates. *Equity & Excellence in Education, 47*(3), 289–304.

Milner, IV, H. R. (2012). Beyond a test score: Explaining opportunity gaps in educational practice. *Journal of Black Studies, 43*(6), 693–718.

Milner, IV, H. R. (2010). What does teacher education have to do with teaching? Implications for diversity studies. *Journal of Teacher Education, 61*(1–2), 118–131.

Milner, IV, H. R., & Howard, T. C. (2013). Counter-narrative as method: Race, policy and research for teacher education. *Race Ethnicity and Education, 16*(4), 536–561.

Mosley, M. (2010). 'That really hit me hard': Moving beyond passive anti-racism to engage with critical race literacy pedagogy. *Race Ethnicity and Education, 13*(4), 449–471.

National Policy Board for Educational Administration. (2015). *Professional Standards for Educational Leaders 2015.* Reston, VA: Author. Retrieved from http://npbea.org/wpcontent/uploads/2017/06/Professional-Standards-for-Educational-Leaders_2015.pdf

No Child Left Behind (NCLB) Act of 2001, Pub. L. No. 107-110, § 115, Stat. 1425 (2002).

Ohito, E. O. (2016). Making the emperor's new clothes visible in anti-racist teacher education: Enacting a pedagogy of discomfort with white preservice teachers. *Equity & Excellence in Education, 49*(4), 454–467.

Picower, B., & Mayorga, E. (Eds.). (2015). *What's race got to do with it? How current school reform policy maintains racial and economic inequality*. New York: Peter Lang Publishing, Inc.

Pollock, M. (Ed.). (2008). *Everyday anti-racism: Getting real about race in schools*. New York: The New Press.

Pollock, M. (2010, winter). Engaging race issues with colleagues: Strengthening our professional communities through everyday inquiry. *Massachusetts Association of Supervision and Curriculum Development (MASCD) Perspectives*.

Raby, R. (2004). 'There's no racism at my school, it's just joking around': Ramifications for anti-racist education. *Race Ethnicity and Education, 7*(4), 367–383.

Rallis, S., Rossman, G., Reagan, T., Cobb, C., & Kuntz, A. (2008). *Leading dynamic schools: How to create and implement ethical policies*. Thousand Oaks, CA: Corwin Press.

Rothstein, R. (2017). *The color of law: A forgotten history of how our government segregated America*. New York: Liveright Publishing Co.

Ryan, J. (2012). *Struggling for inclusion: Educational leadership in a neoliberal world*. Charlotte, NC: Information Age Publishing, Inc.

Scott, J., & Holme, J. J. (2016). The political economy of market-based educational policies: Race and reform in urban school districts, 1915 to 2016. *Review of Research in Education, 40*(1), 250–295.

Sleeter, C. E. (2014). Multiculturalism and education for citizenship in a context of neoliberalism. *Intercultural Education, 25*(2), 85–94.

Strauss, V. (2016, December 8). A sobering look at what Betsy DeVos did to education in Michigan – and what she might do as secretary of education. *The Washington Post*. Retrieved from https://www.washingtonpost.com/news/answer-sheet/wp/2016/12/08/a-sobering-look-at-what-betsy-devos-did-to-education-in-michigan-and-what-she-might-do-as-secretary-of-education/?utm_term=.01516338b1e8

Swanson, J., & Welton, A. (2019). When good intentions only go so far: White principals leading discussions about race. *Urban Education, 54*(5), 732–759.

Ullucci, K. (2011). Learning to see: The development of race and class consciousness in white teachers. *Race Ethnicity and Education, 14*(4), 561–577.

United States Department of Education. (2009). *Race to the Top executive summary*. Washington, D.C.: U.S. Government Printing Office.

United States National Commission on Excellence in Education. (1983). *A nation at risk: The imperative for educational reform*. Washington, D.C.: The National Commission on Excellence in Education.

View, J. L., DeMulder, E., Stribling, S., Dodman, S., Ra, S., Hall, B., & Swalwell, K. (2016). Equity audit: A teacher leadership tool for nurturing teacher research. *The Educational Forum, 80*(4), 380–393.

The Wallace Foundation. (2013). *The principal as school leader: Guiding schools to better teaching and learning*. Retrieved from www.wallacefoundation.org/knowledge-center/Pages/The-School-Principal-as-Leader-Guiding-Schools-to-Better-Teaching-and-Learning.aspx

Welton, A. D., & Diem, S. (2016, February 15). Who will be "My Brother's Keeper?": The problematic nature of using a colorblind approach to address racial inequities. *Teachers College Record.* Retrieved from www.tcrecord.org/content.asp?contentid=19455

Welton, A. D., Diem, S., & Holme, J. J. (2015). Color conscious, cultural blindness: Suburban school districts and demographic change. *Education and Urban Society, 47*(6), 695–722.

Welton, A. D., Harris, T. O., La Londe, P. G., & Moyer, R. T. (2015). Social justice education in a diverse classroom: Examining high school discussions about race, power, and privilege. *Equity & Excellence in Education, 48*(4), 549–570.

Young, M. D., & Laible, J. (2000). White racism, antiracism, and school leader preparation. *Journal of School Leadership, 10*(5), 374–415.

Chapter 2

How School Leaders Respond to Demographic Change

Communities across the United States have experienced significant demographic shifts over the past several decades and the country is becoming more racially and ethnically diverse. While the country's population is still comprised of a majority of white individuals, the share of the white population is declining as other populations, primarily Latinxs, are growing. Indeed, the Pew Research Center projects that the Latinx population will be the largest racial or ethnic majority eligible voting group in the 2020 U.S. presidential election, surpassing Black voters for the first time (Cilluffo & Cohn, 2019).

When we look at where Americans are living across the country, we can see that the majority (175 million) live in small metropolitan areas or suburbs while 98 million live in urban areas and 46 million call rural areas home (Parker et al., 2018). The population growth occurring in suburban and small metropolitan areas is due in larger part to the shifts in demographics. Suburban areas are more racially diverse and are home to a growing number of low-income individuals (Frey, 2011; Kneebone & Garr, 2010). Residents from urban and rural areas are also moving into these areas, as well as immigrants from outside of the United States (Frey, Berube, Singer, & Wilson, 2009; Parker et al., 2018). The majority of the population growth that has occurred across the U.S. over the last 55 years has been a result of immigrants who tend to live more in cities and suburbs. In fact, there are fewer U.S. born individuals living in rural areas today as compared to 20 years ago, and more people are leaving rural areas than moving in (Cilluffo & Cohn, 2019; Parker et al., 2018).

The growing gentrification occurring across U.S. metropolitan areas is also playing a role in changes to the demographic make-up of central cities. As more white individuals move to central cities, low-income people of color are displaced from communities they have long called home (Maciag, 2015). While recent gentrification is still relatively confined to a select group of large U.S. cities, some of whom began experiencing gentrification decades ago, it is still important to monitor as research shows that gentrification is related to demographic changes occurring in schools (Billingham, 2019). Indeed, Frankenberg and colleagues (2019) note that gentrifying cities along with suburban areas are on the frontlines of racial change and, as such, are areas of critical importance when it comes to policy addressing demographic change and diversity within schools.

When we look at the current make-up of public schools, we can also see a shifting demographic landscape. Public school enrollment in the U.S. is not only growing in size but it is also serving a more racially diverse and multiracial student population. From 2000–2016, the number of students attending public schools increased by 7%, surpassing an enrollment number of 50 million (de Bray et al., 2019). In the 2014–15 school year, white students made up less than 50% of the population for the first time in U.S. public schools (McFarland et al., 2019), although they have been the minority for quite some time in schools in the western and southern regions of the country (Frankenberg et al., 2019). At the same time, the number of Latinx students has been steadily increasing while the number of Black, Asian, American Indian/Alaska Native, and multiracial students has remained relatively the same (McFarland et al., 2019) (see Table 2.1).

Despite the demographic shifts occurring and the increase in student racial diversity, schools are growing increasingly segregated across all communities. White and Latinx students are the most racially segregated groups in schools. White students are more likely to attend schools where 69% of the population is white while Latinx students are likely to attend schools where 55% of the population is Latinx. Black students attend schools where almost half of the population is Black, and Asian students are in schools where about a quarter of the population is Asian (Frankenberg et al., 2019).

School segregation is also evident in suburban schools. Black and Latinx students in the suburbs are likely to attend a school that is about 75% nonwhite while white students in suburban schools are likely to attend schools that are 67% white (Frankenberg et al., 2019).

Table 2.1 Number and percentage of students enrolled in PK-12 grade by race, fall 2000–2027

	2000	2015	2027 (projected)
White	28,878,000 (61%)	24,644,000 (49%)	23,274,000 (45%)
Black	8,100,000 (17%)	7,784,000 (15%)	7,888,000 (15%)
Latinx	7,726,000 (16%)	13,080,000 (26%)	15,209,000 (29%)
Asian/Pacific Islander	1,950,000 (4%)	2,697,000 (5%)	3,271,000 (6%)
American Indian/Alaska Native	550,000 (1%)	510,000 (1%)	457,000 (1%)
Two or More Races	N/A	1,723,000 (3%)	1,960,000 (4%)

Source: U.S. Department of Education, National Center for Education Statistics, Common Core of Data (2017)

Rural schools are also highly segregated. White students in rural areas are likely to attend schools that are 80% white while Black and Latinx students in rural areas attend schools that are 57% nonwhite (Frankenberg et al., 2019).

Schools that are racially segregated also tend to be economically segregated. Although an imperfect measure of poverty (Harwell & LeBeau, 2010), eligibility for free/reduced price lunch shows us that Black and Latinx students are more likely to attend schools with more low-income students (Frankenberg et al., 2019).

GLOBAL AND NATIONAL POLITICAL DISCOURSES AROUND WHITE SUPREMACY AND THEIR INFLUENCE ON HOW WE VIEW RACIAL DIVERSITY

The economic foundation of the United States was built by the sacrifice, toil, and labor of immigrants who arrived in this nation either seeking asylum from oppression or in search of the American Dream, and of course Africans who were enslaved and brought to the country involuntarily. However, when politicians like Trump and former President Reagan use the phrase "Make America Great Again" they are not referring to populations indigenous to America such as Native American, Alaska Native, Chicanx and Mexican-Americans, or the history of ethnic immigrants who also represent a foundational fabric of our nation. Instead, there is a collective pining for an America that is rooted in our white colonial past and present, white supremacy, and a white mythology about what it means to be an American who aspires to ascend the racial hierarchy to whiteness (see Kendi, 2016; Omi & Winant, 2015).

This constant barrage of white folklore comes directly from the mouths of our elected officials. For example, Trump's comments on the violent white nationalist rally in Charlottesville in 2017 when he claimed that there were "very fine people on both sides" and there are "two sides to a story" in terms of who is to blame, plus the numerous times he has publicly called Mexican immigrants "rapists" and used derogatory language when describing immigrants from African countries or origins. Now, with the rise of social media, white folklore is easily consumed and then passed on in conversations amongst family members, friends, and neighbors. Thus, our national, and even global political spectacles like Brexit, the rise of white nationalism in Europe, and attacks on Jewish and Islamic places of worship in the U.S. and even New Zealand, mean that our collective responses to the diversifying of our communities is rooted in xenophobia, Islamophobia, anti-Semitism, and white resentment and fear of losing out to diversity.

In our previous research we called district and school communities' responses to becoming increasingly diverse 'colorblindness' (see Welton et al., 2015), for which our now preferred term is 'color-evasiveness'. However, even color-evasiveness may constitute terminology that is too sanitized to describe our current sociopolitical context where the structures and policies serving racism seem very intentional (see Kendi, 2016). Although Trump continues to use very overtly racist sentiments and political spin to push his nationalist agenda, this rising tide of intentional racism was gaining traction prior to his election, and even had a stronghold during the supposed "post-racial" historical moment when we elected our first Black president.

For example, in our research on a racially diversifying suburban school district in the San Antonio, Texas metropolitan area, data which we collected during Obama's first term as president, central office leaders spoke of how the Tea Party movement was gaining traction in their community and had significant influence on the racial discourse and politics among some of the white residents in their district (Holme, Welton, & Diem, 2012). The Tea Party sees itself as a grassroots movement that safeguards free-market ideals like anti-tax, anti-government, and anti-regulation. And although this movement had been in the making since the early 1990s, it officially came to the fore during Obama's first presidential term (Nesbit, 2016).

It is said that even Obama's speeches during his presidency appealed to whiteness by publicly admonishing Blacks (Haney-López, 2014), like in the unveiling of his My Brother's Keeper initiative where he used language that seemed to blame young men of color for the racial oppression they face, but did not point enough blame towards how social and education systems have failed them (Welton & Diem, 2016). Thus, white supremacy is a bipartisan phenomenon, as leaders across the political spectrum have contributed to its maintenance. In education policy we are grappling with how to eliminate the school-to-prison pipeline and dehumanizing ways in which we discipline Black and Brown children in schools (see Crenshaw, Ocen, Nanda, & Carranza, 2015; Morris, 2016). And it can only be assumed that educators' punitive actions towards Black and Brown youth in the classroom can be linked to our policing of Black and Brown bodies nationally, starting with former President Clinton's support of the federal "three strikes" law that increased incarceration rates in the U.S. Clinton also cut social welfare programs like the Aid to Families with Dependent Children to publicly demonstrate that he was getting tough on African Americans (i.e., "welfare queens") dependent upon government assistance (Haney-López, 2014). Thus, we have never had a post-racial moment in the political sphere, and so an undercurrent of white supremacy has always remained a fixture in our American policy consciousness. Given how racially minoritized groups are debased in American political discourse, it is inevitable that these racist views are constructing how educators and other local school actors view and address the diversifying of their communities.

HOW EDUCATIONAL LEADERS RESPOND TO RACIAL DIVERSITY BASED ON THE POLICY CONTEXT

The research on educational leaders' response to the growing diversity in their districts and schools reveals how our current global political context, driven by whiteness and white supremacy, socializes us and affects our daily sentiments, structures, and practices in schools. We have written previously about how educational leaders and their district and school communities are influenced by various nested policy contexts (Diem et al., 2016; Weaver-Hightower, 2008). Policies and associated policy discourses are perceived, received, and enacted through an ecological system of nested policy contexts at the global, national, state, and local level (Weaver-Hightower, 2008). According to Weaver-Hightower (2008) these nested policy contexts serve as a "web of influence" where the state establishes its policy intentions in writing, the policy is then recontextualized to other organizational entities such as state education agencies and school districts, and then finally, local actors like school administrators and teachers reinterpret the policy and determine how to distribute decision-making power in the policy implementation process (Diem et al., 2016; Weaver-Hightower, 2008, p. 158). Nevertheless, the process of how policies and subsequent policy discourses are framed and then reframed at various contextual levels of the policy environment is in no way linear and, indeed, complex. Yet, what we have found in the research on district and school community responses to racial diversity is that when states design policies that are intentionally race-neutral, local policy actors are influenced by the messages coming from their policy environment and intrinsically follow suit with race-neutral attitudes, structures, and practices (Diem et al., 2016; Welton et al., 2015).

To understand how the racial discourses in the policy environment shaped suburban district and school policy actors' responses to increasing racial diversity in their communities, we compared suburban districts in three different metropolitan contexts: San Antonio, Texas; Los Angeles, California; and Minneapolis, Minnesota. Each metropolitan context had key state policies that largely influenced the racial politics of the suburban districts we studied. Texas was and still is largely influenced by high-stakes testing, and its accountability system was highly influential in the Bush Administration's design of No Child Left Behind (NCLB). Texas has also been a legal battle ground over the discrimination against English learners (EL), and an outcome of these court rulings is that now districts are required to provide bilingual instruction for EL students in the elementary grades (Gándara & Rumberger, 2009). California, in contrast, has designed policies that intentionally disregard both race and language. In 1996, the California legislature passed Proposition 209 which amended the state constitution to preclude state agencies from considering race, ethnicity, and sex in public employment, contracts, and education (Contreras, 2005). Essentially, Proposition 209 was an anti-affirmative action policy that greatly limited Black and Brown student access to University of California institutions. Proposition 227 is a subtractive language policy passed in 1998 that eliminated bilingual education in California and required non-native English speakers to receive instruction in a separate English-only class setting. Finally, Minnesota, up until 1999, had statewide enforced desegregation, while integration remained voluntary through inter- and intra-district school choice (Diem et al., 2016). The state is currently being sued by families arguing that an unequal education system has been established by allowing segregation to exist across school districts (*Cruz-Guzman v. Minnesota*, 2018).

Ultimately, we found that the state policy contexts that the districts we studied were situated in was concomitant with how they responded to the expanding racial diversity in their communities. In the suburban San Antonio district, the high-stakes-testing-driven accountability system prompted a significant focus on counting the performance of racial and ethnic student sub-groups. While race mattered in terms of fulfilling mandated state accountability measures, efforts to be culturally responsive to their growing racially diverse student populations were superficial and merely for educators to avoid cultural conflicts with and behavior problems from students. Also, we found that while the district and school leaders restructured their educational services to address these changing demographics, they used race-neutral approaches that reinforce deficit thinking and thus dehumanize students' of color learning experiences (Welton et al., 2015).

Educational leaders in the suburban Los Angeles (LA) district were faced with operating in a state with anti-bilingual and racially hostile policies, and these leaders were the weakest of the three suburban districts we studied in terms of their efforts to be race-conscious. Educators in the suburban LA district were also quick to essentialize racial minoritized groups instead of recognizing the funds of knowledge and cultural wealth these students and their families possess that would be a valued asset to school policymaking and curricular and instructional practices. In contrast, the suburban Minneapolis district we studied was more race-conscious because the former state-desegregation rule put funding and resources towards racial equity efforts, and so the district used these resources for professional development and continuous improvement work in cultural competency. This capacity building and development of more racially equitable practices also prompted district leadership to push their school level leaders to examine their data for racially exclusionary practices in school discipline and to be more forthcoming about how school structures and practices perpetuate the racial achievement gap (Diem et al., 2016). Consequently, we found in each case that educators' responses to the demographic changes occurring in their district communities were a reflection of their state policy context.

WHITENESS AS PROPERTY AND RESISTANCE TO DEMOGRAPHIC CHANGE

Much of the research on district and school community responses to demographic change examines how educational leaders, teachers, and even families may espouse color-evasive perspectives that downplay the significance of race, or claim that they "don't see color or race," but their actions are very much so racialized (Cooper, 2009; Evans, 2007a, 2007b; Turner, 2015). Some of these racialized responses came in the form of educational leaders avoiding any forthcoming discussions about or deeply wrestling with race as a district or school community and instead implementing superficial initiatives like multicultural programs and celebrations, or one-off diversity workshops or professional development that was never applied to practice (Cooper, 2009; Welton et al., 2015). We interpret these types of responses to demographic change where educators and community members avoid addressing race as one form of resistance to change that allows the status quo to safely remain intact. According to Gorski (2019), these experiential diversity initiatives are one way in which white people can "opt out" of having to learn about racism and instead do what is most comfortable to them (p. 59). So, then, white people "opt out of considering racial justice while deriving social and cultural benefits from diversity awareness. It creates the illusion of appreciation while entrenching inequity" (Gorski, 2019, p. 59).

However, much of the resistance to demographic change documented in the research is what could be considered as *whiteness as property*, where the growing numbers of racially diverse students and families joining a district and or school community are seen by white, upper middle-class, and affluent families as a potential encroachment on their property rights (see Harris, 1995). This whiteness as property has manifested as white flight, where white families of economic means see the increase of students and families of color in their communities as a sign that their schools and homes will soon be devalued (Holme, 2002; Holme et al., 2012). Moreover, in recent years, white families have resurrected a tactic once used post-*Brown v. Board of Education* (1954) to avoid desegregation—school district secession—to once again resist racially diverse school settings. In school district secession, white and affluent families siphon themselves off from larger, county-wide school districts in their communities to create their own districts under the race-neutral guise of local control and greater autonomy over decision-making (Siegel-Hawley, Diem, & Frankenberg, 2018). Yet, research shows that school district secession and the creation of new school district boundaries is contributing to increasing levels of school segregation (Frankenberg, Siegel-Hawley, & Diem, 2017; Taylor, Frankenberg, & Siegel-Hawley, 2019).

In our case study on the suburban school district in the San Antonio metropolitan area, as some schools in the district became more racially and socioeconomically diverse, white and middle-class families would move out of the area to neighborhoods with more affluent schools (Holme et al., 2013). Some of the more affluent schools were even located in neighborhoods *within* the district and as white families continued to move north, the district would build new schools to accommodate them (Holme et al., 2012). School choice also precipitated white flight. White and middle-class families would use open choice to transfer to a different school, especially if the neighborhood school's demographics changed to a Title I designation. As a PTA president of an elementary school in the district described:

> I think just the wording of it, Title I scared them that they needed to move out of that area…Or they have done School of Choice. I know they pretty much can't sell their homes right now, but I know that some of them have done you know, changed [using] School of Choice. And it's not—and all of them said it's not anything to do with a bad experience as far as teacher wise or anything, but [it's] demographics.
> (Holme et al., 2013, p. 125)

However, white, middle class, and affluent families aren't just fleeing low-income, racially diversifying school communities; now there is also evidence of white flight from middle-class, racially diversifying suburbs, coined as *ethnoburbs* (Enjeti, 2016; Kye, 2018). For example, Enjeti (2016) described the sentiments of white community members who fled an ethnoburb in suburban Atlanta that over time had an influx of Asian families. The district was strong in terms of its academic offerings and resources, but still white parents, based on the minority stereotype of Asian students, feared the competition their children would face as a result of the growing Asian student population. As one parent candidly shared, "The high school is too competitive, my kids won't get into a good college because of all of the Asians" (Enjeti, 2016, para. 10). As a result, white parents fled well-resourced schools because they were threatened by what opportunities students of color and their families might take away from them.

CONCLUSION

"Critical awareness of racial meanings" (Turner, 2015, p. 33) around school reform may better allow for school leaders to be able to address and serve the growing diversity of students enrolled in public schools. This is particularly important in a color-evasive, market-oriented educational context that ignores persistent racial discrimination and makes it challenging for educators to provide equitable educational opportunities in their districts, schools, and classrooms. Moreover, what is needed is anti-racist leadership: school leaders who are willing to engage in the racial politics that come with demographic change by countering pushback and resistance, i.e., whiteness, from white, middle-class, and affluent stakeholders, because capitulating to white resistance only further delays achieving racial equity and reconciliation for students and families of color.

DISCUSSION QUESTIONS

1. How has the population changed in your school community over the last 10 years? What has been the response to these changes in terms of policy and practice?
2. How does your school community engage in discussions about race or racial equity? How would you characterize these discussions?
3. In your role as a school leader, what actions can you take to let your staff, faculty, students, families, and community know you value racial equity and support a growing diverse population?
4. What types of ongoing, embedded professional development could you provide to expand the racial literacy and the "critical awareness of racial meanings" (Turner, 2015, p. 33) for each stakeholder group (administrators, teachers, students, families, and community members) in your district?
5. For the sake of achieving racial equity for students and families of color, what risks are you willing to take and coalitions of support would you need to build in order to counter resistance and pushback from white, middle-class, and affluent stakeholders while your district/and or school community undergoes demographic changes?

DEMOGRAPHIC CHANGE RESOURCES

- EdChange: www.edchange.org
- EmbraceRace: www.embracerace.org/
- Equity Literacy Institute: www.equityliteracy.org/
- National Education Association EdJustice: https://neaedjustice.org/racial-justice-is-education-justice/
- National Equity Project: https://nationalequityproject.org/
- National Policy Board for Educational Administration (NPBEA): http://npbea.org/
- Race Forward: www.raceforward.org/
- Southern Education Foundation: www.southerneducation.org/
- U.S. Department of Education Equity Assistance Centers
  - Region I: Center for Education Equity – https://cee-maec.org/ (serves Connecticut, Delaware, Kentucky, Maine, Maryland, Massachusetts, New Hampshire, New Jersey, New York, Pennsylvania, Puerto Rico, Rhode Island, Vermont, Virgin Islands, West Virginia)
  - Region II: South Central Collaborative for Equity – www.idra.org/
    (serves Alabama, Arkansas, District of Columbia, Florida, Georgia, Louisiana, Mississippi, North Carolina, South Carolina, Tennessee, Texas, Virginia)
  - Region III: Midwest and Plains Equity Assistance Center – https://greatlakesequity.org/
    (serves Illinois, Indiana, Iowa, Kansas, Michigan, Minnesota, Missouri, Nebraska, North Dakota, Ohio, Oklahoma, South Dakota, Wisconsin)
  - Region IV: Western Educational Equity Assistance Center – https://msudenver.edu/weeac/
    (serves Alaska, American Samoa, Arizona, California, Colorado, Commonwealth of the Northern Mariana Islands, Guam, Hawaii, Idaho, Montana, Nevada, New Mexico, Oregon, Utah, Washington, Wyoming)

RECOMMENDED READINGS

Frankenberg, E., & Orfield, O. (Eds.). (2012). *The resegregation of suburban schools: A hidden crisis in American Education.* Cambridge, MA: Harvard Education Press.

Gorski, P. (2019). Avoiding racial equity detours. *Educational Leadership, 76*(7), 56–61.
Lewis, A., & Diamond, J. B. (2015). *Despite the best intentions: How racial inequality thrives in good schools.* New York: Oxford University Press.
Rothstein, R. (2017). *The color of law: A forgotten history of how our government segregated America.* New York: Liveright Publishing Corporation.
Turner, E. O. (2020). *Suddenly diverse: How school districts manage race and inequality.* Chicago, IL: University of Chicago Press.

REFERENCES

Billingham, C. (2019). Within-district racial segregation and the elusiveness of white student return to urban public schools. *Urban Education, 54*(2), 151–181.
Cilluffo, A., & Cohn, D. (2019, April 11). 6 demographic trends shaping the U.S. and the world in 2019. *Pew Research Center.* Retrieved from www.pewresearch.org/fact-tank/2019/04/11/6-demographic-trends-shaping-the-u-s-and-the-world-in-2019/
Contreras, F. E. (2005). The reconstruction of merit post-proposition 209. *Educational Policy, 19*(2), 371–395.
Cooper, C. W. (2009). Performing cultural work in demographically changing schools: Implications for expanding transformative leadership frameworks. *Educational Administration Quarterly, 45*(5), 694–724.
Crenshaw, K., Ocen, P., Nanda, J., & Carranza, T. (2015). *Black girls matter: Pushed out, overpoliced, and underprotected.* Columbia Law School, Center for Intersectionality and Social Policy Studies, African American Policy Forum.
Cruz-Guzman v. Minnesota, A16-1265 Supreme Court (2018).
de Bray, C., Musu, L., McFarland, J., Wilkinson-Flicker, S., Diliberti, M., Zhang, A., Branstetter, C., & Wang, X. (2019). *Status and trends in the education of racial and ethnic groups 2018* (NCES 2019–038). U.S. Department of Education. Washington, D.C.: National Center for Education Statistics. Retrieved from https://nces.ed.gov/pubsearch/
Diem, S., Welton, A. D., Frankenberg, E., & Holme, J. J. (2016). Racial diversity in the suburbs: How race-neutral responses to demographic change perpetuate inequity in suburban school districts. *Race Ethnicity and Education, 19*(4), 731–762.
Enjeti, A. (August 25, 2016). Ghost of white people past: Witnessing white flight from an Asian ethnoburb. *Pacific Standard.* Retrieved from https://psmag.com/news/ghosts-of-white-people-past-witnessing-white-flight-from-an-asian-ethnoburb
Evans, A. E. (2007a). Changing faces: Suburban school responses to demographic change. *Education and Urban Society, 39*(3), 315–348.

Evans, A. E. (2007b). School leaders and their sensemaking about race and demographic change. *Educational Administration Quarterly, 43*(2), 159–188.

Frankenberg, E., Ee, J., Ayscue, J. B., & Orfield, G. (2019). *Harming our common future: America's segregated schools 65 years after Brown.* Los Angeles, CA: The Civil Rights Project/Proyecto Derechos Civiles and Center for Education and Civil Rights.

Frankenberg, E., Siegel-Hawley, G., & Diem, S. (2017). Segregation by district boundary line: The fragmentation of Memphis area schools. *Educational Researcher, 46*(8), 449–463.

Frey, W. H. (2011, May). *Melting pot cities and suburbs: Racial and ethnic change in metro America in the 2000s.* Washington, D.C.: The Brookings Institution.

Frey, W. H., Berube, A., Singer, A., & Wilson, J. H. (2009). *Getting current: Recent demographic trends in metropolitan America.* Washington, D.C.: Brookings Institution Metropolitan Policy Program.

Gándara, P. & Rumberger, R. (2009). Immigration, language, and education: How does language policy structure opportunity? *Teachers College Record, 111*(3), 750–782.

Gorski, P. (2019). Avoiding racial equity detours. *Educational Leadership, 76*(7), 56–61.

Haney-López, I. (2014). *Dog whistle politics: how coded racial appeals have reinvented racism and wrecked the middle class.* Oxford; New York: Oxford University Press.

Harris, C. (1995). Whiteness as property. In K. Crenshaw, N. Gotanda, G. Peller, & K. Thomas (Eds.), *Critical race theory: The key writings that formed the movement* (pp. 276–291). New York: The New Press.

Harwell, M., & LeBeau, B. (2010). Student eligibility for a free lunch as an SES measure in education research. *Educational Researcher, 39*(2), 120–131.

Holme, J. J. (2002). Buying homes, buying schools: School choice and the social construction of school quality. *Harvard Educational Review, 72*(2), 177–206.

Holme, J. J., Frankenberg, E., Diem, S. L., & Welton, A. (2013). School choice in suburbia: The impact of choice policies on the potential for suburban integration. *Journal of School Choice, 7*(2), 113–141.

Holme, J. J., Welton, A., & Diem, S. (2012). Pursuing "separate but equal" in suburban Texas: A case study of Southern Independent School District. In E. Frankenberg & G. Orfield (Eds.), *The resegregation of suburban schools* (pp. 45–68). Cambridge, MA: Harvard Education Press.

Kendi, I. X. (2016). *Stamped from the beginning: The definitive history of racist ideas in America.* New York: Nation Books.

Kneebone, E., & Garr, E. (2010, January). *The suburbanization of poverty: Trends in metropolitan America, 2000 to 2008.* Washington, D.C.: The Brookings Institution.

Kye, S. H. (2018). The rise of ethnoburbs. *Contexts, 17*(4), 68–70.

Maciag, M. (2015). Gentrification in America report. *Governing.* Retrieved from www.governing.com/gov-data/gentrification-in-cities-governing-report.html

McFarland, J., Hussar, B., Zhang, J., Wang, X., Wang, K., Hein, S., Diliberti, M., Forrest Cataldi, E., Bullock Mann, F., & Barmer, A. (2019). *The Condition of Education 2019* (NCES 2019–144). U.S. Department of Education. Washington, D.C.: National Center for Education Statistics. Retrieved from https://nces.ed.gov/pubsearch/pubsinfo.asp?pubid=2019144

Morris, M. W. (2016). *Pushout: The criminalization of Black girls in schools.* New York: The New Press.

Nesbit, J. (2016). The secret origins of the Tea Party: How big oil and big tobacco partnered with the Koch brothers to take over the GOP. *Time.* Retrieved from https://time.com/secret-origins-of-the-tea-party/

Omi, M., & Winant, H. (1994). *Racial formation in the United States: From the 1960s to the 1990s* (2nd ed.). New York: Routledge.

Parker, K., Horowitz, J. M., Brown, A., Fry, R., Cohn, D., & Igielnik, R. (2018, May 22). What unites and divides urban, suburban, and rural communities. *Pew Research Center.* Retrieved from www.pewsocialtrends.org/2018/05/22/demographic-and-economic-trends-in-urban-suburban-and-rural-communities/

Siegel-Hawley, G., Diem, S., & Frankenberg, E. (2018). The disintegration of Memphis-Shelby County, Tennessee: School district secession and local control in the 21st century. *American Educational Research Journal, 55*(4), 651–692.

Taylor, K., Frankenberg, E., & Siegel-Hawley, S. (2019). Racial segregation in southern schools, school districts, and counties where districts have seceded. *AERA Open, 5*(3), 1–16.

Turner, E. O. (2015). Districts' responses to demographic change: Making sense of race, class, and immigration in political and organizational context. *American Educational Research Journal, 52*(1), 4–39.

Weaver-Hightower, M. B. (2008). An ecology metaphor for educational policy analysis: A call to complexity. *Educational Researcher, 37*(3), 153–167.

Welton, A. D., & Diem, S. (2016, February 15). Who will be "My Brother's Keeper?": The problematic nature of using a colorblind approach to address racial inequities. *Teachers College Record.* Retrieved from www.tcrecord.org/content.asp?contentid=19455

Welton, A. D., Diem, S., & Holme, J. J. (2015). Color conscious, cultural blindness: Suburban school districts and demographic change. *Education and Urban Society, 47*(6), 695–722.

Chapter 3

School Choice and Who Has a Right to Choose

School choice policies have long been a part of the U.S. education system. They are designed with the intent to give families more options for how their children receive an education. However, these policies are not without their issues, particularly when it comes to equitable educational opportunity. Indeed, school choice policies can either provide schooling environments that are diverse and of high quality or they can work to increase segregation and inequality (Frankenberg, Siegel-Hawley, & Wang, 2011). While at one time school choice policies were used to mitigate segregation and simultaneously provide families with options that did not exclude a school's ability to racially diversify, the current context that seeks to establish education as a market-driven system is making it increasingly difficult to do so (Wells, 2014). Indeed, the rise of market-driven education reforms has created a system that operates as a marketplace of schooling options in which the increase of choice is assumed to lead to higher quality and more efficient and innovative schools. Market-driven school choice policies such as charter schools, vouchers, and open-enrollment programs that are highly racialized have been adopted across the U.S. in conjunction with the current accountability movement, stressing testing and outcomes over equitable access to quality schools (Wells, 2014). Since schools are accountable for how well their students perform on standardized assessments, school choice often results in schools choosing students (those that will help them meet their benchmarks) or implementing strategies that attract higher performing students (Diem, Carpenter, & Lewis-Durham, 2019; Holme, Carkhum & Rangel, 2013; Jabbar, 2015b).

Additionally, despite research that shows how these policies almost always lead to increased racial inequality (Siegel-Hawley, 2016; Wells, 2014), they are growing at a rapid rate.

School choice on its face sounds like an ideal approach to education. Who doesn't want the ability to choose where to send their children to school based on factors most important to them? Yet, in reality school choice is much more complex as, like any other choices in the market, there are differing options (Orfield, 2013) and everybody does not have the same ability and access to choose. Research shows that those benefitting most from school choice policies are families, predominately white and affluent, who have access to resources and networks about their choices (Beal & Hendry, 2012; Fuller, Elmore, & Orfield, 1996; Roda & Wells, 2013; Scott, 2005). Since families differ in terms of their financial means, they differ, too, in whether they can truly consider school choice as an option. This is also coupled with the structural characteristics of the local choice context (e.g., residential segregation, marketplace, commute time to schools) that can affect which students have the ability to move to desired schools (Rich & Jennings, 2015). Moreover, while white and affluent families may claim to value racial diversity in public schools, when it actually comes to choosing schools in which to enroll their children, they select what they believe to be the "best" schools, which are predominately white (Roda & Wells, 2013). This contradictory thinking about racial diversity is representative of a larger societal problem and understanding around how choice actually works, who gets to make choices, and who benefits the most from these choices. The assumption is that in a free marketplace, people should have the ability to choose what is in their best interest and all other tangential factors (e.g., racial segregation in schools) will work themselves out on their own. Moreover, in a market-driven education system that forces schools to compete with each other, schools will feel pressured to increase the quality of education provided, thus educational innovation will increase, better academic outcomes will occur, schools will be more efficient, and inequality will lessen (Feinberg & Lubienski, 2008; Miron & Welner, 2012).

Often what's missing in the school choice conversation is how these policies can serve as a catalyst for segregated or integrated school settings.[1] Moreover, as schools become more unequal, racial and socioeconomic inequalities grow, and failure to meet academic performance levels continues to have devastating impacts on school communities, school leaders need to be cognizant as to how school choice is working and who serves as its greatest beneficiary (Orfield,

2013). Scholars have argued that any conversation around school choice must also include racial diversity and equity or these policies will do nothing to address the rising inequality in our public schools. Of course, this is hard to do in policy environments that fail to place a high value on racial diversity and when, judicially, the courts have retreated on their commitment to ensuring school districts are not operating segregated schools (Clotfelter, 2004). One only needs to turn to the *Parents Involved in Community Schools v. Seattle School District No. 1* (2007) ruling to gain insight into the U.S. Supreme Court's opinion on how to provide racially diverse learning environments. The Court struck down two school districts' voluntary efforts to racially diversify their schools and ruled that schools cannot use race as a sole factor in such efforts. Chief Justice Roberts famously stated in the majority's opinion, "The way to stop discriminating on the basis of race is to stop discriminating on the basis of race" (p. 2768). This color-evasive view of how to go about preventing racially isolated schools without being able to take a student's race into account when doing so has left school districts seeking to create and/or maintain racially diverse schools in a quandary as they do not want to be subject to potential lawsuits. Yet, the Court also left room for school districts to implement various student assignment strategies to achieve diverse school settings, and many districts continue to implement racially conscious student assignment policies that seek to create racially diverse schools and provide families with an array of school choice options (Frankenberg, Anderson, & Taylor, 2017). Recent research has identified 111 school districts as having voluntary integration policies (Kahlenberg, 2016; Potter et al., 2016; Reardon & Owens, 2014). However, when looking at who is actually working to implement such policies to promote diverse student populations, other research has identified only 59 districts working toward this end (Anderson & Frankenberg, 2019). And of these 59 districts implementing integration policies, the majority (46) use socioeconomic status to guide enrollment decisions while a smaller number (13) use race and socioeconomic status to try to diversify their schools (Anderson & Frankenberg, 2019).

In this chapter, we provide a brief history of school choice, including the racialized market-driven agenda behind it and the racial implications of implementing these types of policies for school districts and communities. We highlight a few examples of school choice options that are not only growing in popularity but those that have been available to school districts for decades. We then discuss the relationship between school choice and inequality, illustrating the segregative effect of school choice if not designed in ways that intentionally seek to achieve integrated school settings. We discuss the general school choice discourse existent in policy settings as well as strategies school leaders are utilizing in market-driven contexts to better inform school leaders of the policy debate and arm them with the knowledge necessary to be active participants in school choice deliberations. We conclude the chapter by providing specific examples of school choice policies educational leaders have developed and implemented that are race-conscious, to elucidate the possibilities for achieving equity and racial diversity in a school choice context.

SCHOOL CHOICE AND ITS HISTORICALLY RACIALIZED MARKET-DRIVEN AGENDA

The idea of school choice has been around for over a half a century. Milton Friedman is often cited as the first person to argue for free market principles in education. Some argue that the vision he proposed for how public education should operate, which was based on the freedom to choose and individual rights, was a response to the *Brown v. Board of Education* (1954) decision (Aggarwal, 2015). Indeed, in 1955, just a year after *Brown* and the same year when *Brown II* (1955) was decided, while Friedman condemned segregation he also stated that forced desegregation was infringing on families' right to choose schools that were best suited for their children. He therefore suggested that school choice would be the best way to address both of these issues (Aggarwal, 2015). Yet, in actuality, choice was immediately used after *Brown* (1954) as a means for white families to preserve segregation and avoid school desegregation. Choice plans and vouchers were both used to maintain segregation. White students did not choose to transfer to Black schools and Black students that chose to transfer to white schools found themselves to be small in numbers and far from welcome in their new schools (Orfield, 2013). Freedom of choice plans were also implemented across the South to keep segregation intact. Black students were technically able to attend white schools but those who did were harassed, threatened, and had to jump through a number of hurdles to do so, which dissuaded most Black families from sending their children to these schools in fear of their children's safety (Orfield, 2013). Freedom of choice plans, as a result, left segregated patterns of schooling across southern communities. They also illustrate how race was, and still is, intertwined with school choice.

It was not until a year after the 1964 Civil Rights Act, which outlawed discrimination on the basis of race and color and prohibited racial school segregation, among other issues, that actual guidelines were set around school choice. Included in these guidelines was not just the ability to make choices and that those choices be honored, but that any choices that led to increased segregation were not allowed. Two years later, the Office of Civil Rights and the federal courts began requiring real desegregation instead of school choice plans (Orfield, 2013). Fourteen years after its *Brown* ruling, the U.S. Supreme Court heard a challenge to freedom of choice plans in *Green v. County School Board of New Kent County* (1968) and ruled that such plans would not lead to full desegregation. Rather, desegregation would need to be achieved through a number of factors, what would commonly be known as the "Green factors," including desegregated faculties, staff, facilities, extracurricular activities, and transportation (Orfield & Eaton, 1996). A few years later, the *Swann v. Charlotte-Mecklenburg Board of Education* (1971) ruling approved busing students to schools outside of their neighborhoods as a means to achieve desegregation.

Around the same time as school districts began utilizing busing for desegregation purposes, magnet schools were accepted by federal courts as a feasible school choice option (Smrekar & Goldring, 1999). Magnet schools were located predominately in large cities. Through specialized curricula and theme-based schools, magnets sought to draw white students to enroll in schools with Black students and therefore achieve desegregation without busing (Grooms & Williams, 2015). Indeed, magnet schools were a very successful school choice option that assisted in racially diversifying schools. They have been consistently popular in communities and have been able to expand in large part because of federal aid (Frankenberg & Lee, 2009). During the Obama Administration, when school integration efforts saw a revival after being absent from the federal education policy agenda for years, school districts receiving funding through the Magnet Schools Assistance Program were even encouraged to try to make these options more attractive to their communities to mitigate racial segregation (Siegel-Hawley, 2016). However, in more recent years some have begun to question whether magnet schools are still "magnetizing," particularly in a context where racial diversity has become less of a desired goal in these schools (Christensen et al., 2003).

School choice policies today are far less focused on achieving racial diversity than they are on competition in the marketplace. By the mid-1980s, despite the success of previous policies in addressing racial inequality and lessening the Black-white achievement gap, a new era of education reform took shape that was more interested in academic excellence. The focus shifted to standards and high-stakes accountability as well as free-market school choice policies, neither of which centered racial equity (Wells, 2014). Furthermore, as Wells (2014) argues, these policies over time have become interconnected as the implementation of standards and accountability measures across states has almost always coincided with the implementation of a market-driven school choice policy. For example, the No Child Left Behind Act (NCLB) of 2001 required failing schools, schools whose populations included a majority of students of color and low-income students, to offer students the choice to transfer out of those schools. The policy did nothing in terms of recognizing the root cause of why these schools were failing, which in large part was due to years of being underresourced, and further placed them in precarious situations by letting students transfer to other schools. Families were also allowed to choose to send their children to other public schools if their school was deemed unsafe. NCLB also supported the growth of charter schools, which only increased during the Obama Administration. The Obama Administration's Race to the Top program provided over $4 billion in grant funding to states for comprehensive education reform in six core areas including standards, assessments, and charter schools. Indeed, the expansion of charter schools was one of Obama's key education priorities; the number of students attending charter schools grew by 3% during his tenure (Strauss, 2016).

Charter schools, while still not large in numbers, are the fastest growing school choice policy (Wells, 2014). The original vision for charter schools was conceived in 1988 by Albert Shanker, then-president of the American Federation of Teachers. Shanker envisioned a public school where teachers would have the opportunity to use their expertise and be more actively involved in decision-making processes to create innovative learning environments. Moreover, this vision included bringing together diverse student populations and increasing low-income students' social mobility, as well as unionizing charter schools. Unfortunately, when charter schools began to take shape in the 1990s, they were based on market-driven concepts. Indeed, the vast majority of charter schools today have transformed into competitive sites that families vie for in the open marketplace without consideration placed on fostering racial diversity or teachers' visions for inclusive pedagogical practices (Kahlenberg & Potter, 2014; White, 2015). Yet, they continue to garner support from families of color because the assumption is that charter schools provide better educational options for their children as opposed to the underresourced neighborhood public schools. And while this may be true in many cases, collectively charter schools are not helping all children, and often are actually hurting them (Strauss, 2014).

Charter schools are publicly funded but independently operated. They are particularly appealing because they do not have to manage the same types of regulations placed on traditional public schools, which advocates argue opens them up to more possibilities in how education can be delivered (Diem & Hawkman, 2019). Yet, research shows that these schools are not the innovative spaces they were initially conceived to be, students in these schools are not performing better academically as compared to students in traditional public schools, and in many cases charter schools are more racially segregated (Frankenberg et al., 2011). For example, a recent study concluded that one out of every seven charter schools had a student population that was comprised of at least 99% students of color (Greenblat, 2018).

Open-enrollment plans are another form of school choice that allows students to transfer from one school to another. There are two types of open enrollment policies—inter-district and intra-district—that allow families to choose to send their children to schools outside of their assigned district or within their assigned district, respectively (Miron & Welner, 2013). Research shows that both of these types of school choice options can exacerbate racial segregation and students from low-income families and students of color are least likely to participate in the programs while white and more affluent families are more likely to utilize the programs to transfer their children to better schools (Holme & Wells, 2008; Wells, 2014). Yet, other research shows that when inter-district choice policies are intentionally designed to reduced racial or economic isolation, they can serve as important policy tools for promoting integration (Finnigan et al., 2015; Wells et al., 2009). However, because the programs are choice-based, the success of these policies is very much dependent on whether participating suburban school districts provide space for students from urban school districts to enroll in their schools. Moreover, the context in which these policies are situated can shape how the plans are implemented as well as the level of ongoing political support (Finnigan et al., 2015).

Vouchers are a type of school choice option that first gained significant attention in the years following *Brown* (1954) when school officials in Prince Edward County, Virginia, chose to close its segregated public schools to avoid desegregation. White students were provided private schools vouchers, which they used to attend newly established white schools, while Black students were left for five years without schools where they could attend (Orfield, 2013). While the Supreme Court eventually ruled that Prince Edward County had to reopen its schools (*Griffin v. County School Board of Prince Edward County*, 1964), it became clear that segregation and inequity could be maintained through school vouchers.

Fast forward to 1990, voucher programs again took center stage as the Milwaukee Parental Choice Program was heavily criticized for increasing segregation as the majority of those students utilizing the vouchers were Black and Latinx students. Additionally, the schools in which the students were using their vouchers were inferior, lacked resources, and were not experiencing high academic outcomes (Aggarwal, 2015).

Vouchers are still used today and are issued by the government for students, typically specific groups of students (e.g., low-income students), to use at a private school of their choice (Miron & Welner, 2013). Most recently, Secretary of Education DeVos reignited the voucher debate in her school choice agenda, advocating for the use of public funds for private school vouchers in the name of families having the right to choose, despite the research showing the ineffectiveness of voucher programs (see e.g., Mills & Wolf, 2017; Waddington & Berends, 2018).

SCHOOL CHOICE, INEQUALITY, AND SEGREGATION

Given the racialized history of school choice policies, it is not surprising that choice systems continue to play a role in problems of inequality and segregation. Although racial attitudes have progressed since the initial days of school choice, school districts remain highly segregated and choice, in large part, continues to contribute to inequality. This is important to note as we know from decades of research the harmful effects of school segregation, which is attributed to racially discriminatory policies and structures that were intentionally put in place and that, as a result, depleted resources from segregated spaces (Rothstein, 2017). Indeed, segregated schooling environments face a number of issues that contribute to unequal educational opportunities. They are more likely to have inadequate resources and facilities, less experienced and qualified teachers, and weaker curricular offerings, which all contribute to students' lower academic outcomes (see e.g., Clotfelter, Ladd, & Vigdor, 2010; Orfield & Eaton, 1996; Rumberger & Palardy, 2005;

Welner, 2006). Alternatively, truly integrated schooling environments are associated with better academic and social outcomes. Students who attend desegregated schools are more likely to have cross-racial relationships, less prejudicial attitudes, and are more likely to live in integrated neighborhoods as adults (Mickelson, 2011).

Copious volumes of research show the segregative impact of school choice. Indeed, when school choice policies are color-evasive and not intentionally designed to racially or socioeconomically integrate schools, they lead to segregated schooling environments (Roda & Wells, 2013). Increased levels of racial and economic segregation in large school districts has been attributed to the growth of charter, magnet, and private schools (Saporito & Sohoni, 2006, 2007). Charter schools have been found to be more segregated with student populations that are either predominately white or those that are majority students of color (Frankenberg et al., 2011). Magnet schools are having a harder time realizing the goals of integration that they were initially founded on in part because public interest in racially diverse schools has waned (Smrekar & Honey, 2015).

Moreover, the racial composition of a school continues to play a critical role in families' decisions as to where to enroll their children. White parents are least likely to enroll their children in schools with Black student majorities (Billingham & Hunt, 2016), even if they value racial diversity (Roda & Wells, 2013). Research shows that, on average, the school choices parents make for their children are exacerbating school segregation and unequal educational opportunity (Billingham & Hunt, 2016). Indeed, as Schneider and Buckley (2002) state, "if White parents select schools on the basis of racial makeup regardless of a school's instructional quality or curriculum, the end result could be highly segregated schools chosen on the basis of race and not academic achievement" (p. 134).

Disparities among who participates in school choice also exist. Many school choice policies do not cover transportation. Thus, if public transit options are not readily available and families do not have the means to transport their children to schools they cannot take advantage of such opportunities (Holme et al., 2013). Communities of color may also be limited in their choice options and not guaranteed access to desired schools as this depends on space availability, which may result in families turning to charters and voucher programs for their children. Additionally, some families simply choose schools that are close to their neighborhood even though the school may be segregated (Holme, Diem, & Welton, 2014).

Despite school choice policies' attempt to be color-evasive and therefore, in the eyes of those administering them, "equal" in terms of who has the ability to take advantage of them, they continue to have racialized effects, as evident through the aforementioned discussion. Indeed, as will be considered below, the discourse around school choice perpetuates the false narrative that simply being able to choose a school, for those families that have the option to do so, results in better options for all students. The discourse almost never includes any type of discussion on how an individual choice can impact an entire school community.

GENERAL DISCOURSE THAT PROMOTES SCHOOL CHOICE

School choice policies have always had bipartisan party support. While most Republicans are in favor of all forms of school choice, Democrats are more particular in their types of support (e.g., Democrats may support charter schools but are opposed to voucher programs). Those who support school choice argue that families should have the right to choose where to send their children to school and if schools were run more like businesses and subject to competition, those that are performing better at their "job" would attract more students and those that are not should no longer remain in business. Alternatively, those that oppose school choice argue that the education system is not a business and should not be treated as such. They believe that using public dollars to support school choice undermines the public school system, where the majority of students are enrolled, and by privatizing public education inequitable educational opportunity will abound.

In the Trump era, Secretary of Education Betsy DeVos came right out of the gate pushing for school choice, a cause that has been central to her agenda and career prior to leading the U.S. Department of Education. In the first two years of the Trump Administration, after a tumultuous confirmation process in which Vice President Mike Pence had to cast the tie-breaking vote to confirm her as the Secretary of Education, and despite having control in both the Senate and House of Representatives, DeVos was unable to push through a budget that would cut funding from the U.S. Department of Education and use federal dollars to support private school choice (Meckler, 2018). While DeVos may not be able to obtain the federal funding she desires for her school choice agenda, in local communities and across states choice efforts persist, despite the persistent inequities associated with them.

SCHOOL CHOICE AND EDUCATIONAL LEADERSHIP

School leaders bear the brunt of market-driven policies like school choice. In an increasingly competitive education environment with pressures to maintain or increase student enrollment and navigate accountability policies, school leaders must employ strategies that attract families to their schools, many of which have implications for racial equity. For instance, according to Jabbar (2015a), "If schools do not respond to such pressures and improve academics, they risk losing the funding that accompanies each student, and their school might be closed. Schools must therefore compete to survive" (p. 1094). In contexts where school districts are competing with different school choice policies at the same time, this is of particular concern as enrollment can fall and schools may eventually have to shut their doors.

In order to be competitive in the current education marketplace, school leaders must have a working understanding of the market and be able to recognize market pressures. School leaders should be aware of the impacts of school choice (e.g., losing students to charter schools) so they can respond appropriately. In her research of school choice in New Orleans, Jabbar (2015a, 2015b) found that the characteristics of a school leader as well as their perceptions and understanding of the marketplace play a critical role in the school choice process. That is, the strategies they chose to employ in the marketplace were impacted by their perceptions of their school's position in the marketplace hierarchy and the level of competition for their school. These findings support research by Jennings (2010) who found that principals' biographies and how they made sense of accountability systems and school choice play a critical role in student admissions. Additionally, Turner's (2018) research on how race and context influence school districts' marketing decisions shows that strategies taken to attract families to schools were also heavily influenced by how they viewed themselves in the marketplace. It is therefore important to understand how school leaders are perceiving competition, as they are ultimately the ones that implement school choice policies, as well as to understand the local context and who are thought of as "rivals" in the marketplace (Jabbar, 2015a).

We also argue that school leaders need to be cognizant of the role of race in the marketplace and how school choice and race are intertwined and impact leaders' strategies and responses. Turner (2018) explores the racialization of competition and marketing in her research and finds that when school district leaders engage in strategies to market racial diversity as a way to attract families to their schools, this is often done in order to attract and maintain affluent and middle-class white families. Specifically, school leaders were "selling" the idea of how white students would accumulate more capital by being in schools with students of color suggesting "that the representations and presence of people of color can come to be seen as valuable in a White dominated society while nonetheless reifying whiteness, creating new privileges for upper- and middle-class White children…" (Turner, 2018, p. 20). In turn, this selling of diversity may result in schools perhaps being more diverse but it does nothing to address the racialized marketplace in which these strategies are employed.

SCHOOL CHOICE PLANS THAT CENTER RACE AND RACIAL EQUITY

School leaders "are expected to be the key drivers of competitive strategies in a decentralized choice setting" (Jabbar, 2015a, p. 1101). At the same time, they also need to make sure that whatever strategies they are implementing are racially conscious, inclusive, and less competitive, if we truly seek to create racially diverse schools. Yet, not all school leaders are aware of the strategies that can work to this end and make them competitive in the marketplace. We offer a few examples of school choice options available to school leaders that center race and racial equity that we believe, when implemented appropriately, can lead to more equitable educational opportunities for all students. It is important to note that in all of the examples we discuss, it is never enough to think that "diversifying" schools and placing Black, Brown, and white students in the same building is the magic bullet to achieving racial equity. We must also continuously invest resources in communities and support the cultural assets students bring with them to the classroom every day. Perhaps had we supported the strengths of Black schools prior to desegregation efforts, our education system might currently be in a very different place.

Controlled-Choice Student Assignment

Controlled-choice student assignment plans offer families structured choice options that can both work to provide choice and racially diversify schools. These plans can be district-wide and open up choices across the entire district, or the district can be divided up into different geographic zones and choice is provided within specific zones (Diem,

2012). Successful controlled-choice plans require clearly defined parameters: goals must be set for diverse student enrollment with demographic data considered, constantly monitored, and updated in any algorithms used to assign students to schools; and the majority of families need to receive their first choice in order to get buy in from the community (Quick, 2016b). The Berkeley Unified School District (Berkeley, CA) has been implementing an iteration of a controlled-choice student assignment plan since 1995 with the goal of achieving integrated schools and providing families with choices. Specifically, the district uses a composite diversity map that looks at parent education level, parent income level, and race and ethnicity in the city's 445 planning areas. Each area is assigned a diversity composite category of 1–3 based on the three aforementioned diversity factors. Students are then assigned to schools based on the diversity category number assigned to the planning area where they reside, along with their choice preferences. Students who reside in a specific attendance zone are also given priority to attend schools in their zones. The district monitors the plan regularly to see if changes need to be made to ensure schools are maintaining the district's diversity goals (BUSD, 2019; Diem, 2012).

Diverse-by-Design Charter Schools

While still relatively small in number, diverse-by-design charter schools are popping up across the U.S. with the goal of creating racially and socioeconomically diverse schooling environments. While research shows that, left to the open marketplace, charter schools contribute to school segregation, when designed with racial and socioeconomic diversity in mind, they may be able to do just the opposite and provide diverse school settings (Potter & Quick, 2018). In Rhode Island, Blackstone Valley Prep enrolls students from four racially and socioeconomically diverse communities, utilizes a culturally responsive curriculum reflective of its students' backgrounds, and does not separate students in classes based on performance. Teachers are also provided with professional development opportunities in which they reflect upon their positionalities and biases as well as larger societal inequities. Students in the diverse charter school are performing well academically and applications are over six times the number of students the school can serve. Yet, as the demographics in the communities change, some becoming more low-income, there is a fear that the school will become less diverse (Zimmer, 2018). This is also the case at City Garden Montessori School in St. Louis, Missouri, another diverse-by-design charter school that provides free and diverse Montessori education to children who live in nearby neighborhoods. While the demographics in the catchment zone where the school draws its students was initially one of the most racially and socioeconomically diverse parts of St. Louis, it is becoming less so as neighborhoods are gentrifying (Quick, 2018). However, school leaders in City Garden are determined to make changes necessary to maintain its diverse enrollment by engaging with and recruiting low-income families and those of color as well as lobbying the state legislature to be able to use a weighted lottery system in their admissions process so they can guarantee a specific number of low-income student seats in the school (Quick, 2018).

Magnet Schools

One of the oldest forms of school choice, when designed appropriately magnet schools are still very much one of the viable options available to school leaders to racially diversify their schools. In a marketplace that is proliferating with school choice options, magnet schools distinguish themselves as being the form of school choice that was intentionally designed for the purpose of racial integration (Frankenberg & Siegel-Hawley, 2008). Yet, school leaders must also ensure that the strategies they utilize in their magnet programs take into consideration a range of factors to avoid the potential of racially isolating students. Strategies such as weighted lottery systems, regularly monitoring neighborhood demographic changes and making sure student enrollment is reflective of these changes, and avoiding standalone magnet programs within larger schools that split up the larger school (with the magnet element often racially identifiable) can work to racially diversify magnet schools (Frankenberg & Siegel-Hawley, 2008; Holme, Frankenberg, Diem, & Welton, 2013). Hartford Public Schools (Hartford, CT) utilizes an inter-district magnet program that resulted from a settlement in *Sheff v. O'Neill* (1996), where the lead plaintiff, a fourth grader at the time of the initial litigation, was arguing for equitable and integrated education for children living in Hartford and the surrounding suburban areas. The program enrolls students from Hartford Public Schools and suburban districts; there is also an open choice program that allows students to transfer from school districts. The magnet schools, of which there are approximately 45, are operated by the district and the Capitol Region Education Council (CREC), a Regional Educational Service Center in Connecticut. The Hartford School Choice Office administers the program and uses a lottery system to meet its diversity goal: almost half of the students of color from Hartford will attend more racially diverse schools. The magnet program has been successful both in terms of achieving racially and socioeconomically integrated student populations as well as positive academic outcomes (Quick, 2016a).

Regional Equity Plans

Regional policies outside of education have long been in existence to connect cities and suburbs to provide shared services such as transit and housing to reduce racial segregation between municipalities (Finnigan & Holme, 2015). While these policies have not been implemented at any kind of significant level, particularly in the education arena, they can still be looked to as a means to reduce racial isolation and provide families with choice. Typically referred to as inter-district school integration plans, these voluntary regional choice plans have been around since the 1960s yet are implemented only in 13 metropolitan areas across 10 states. The programs are consistently popular but due to funding and accountability issues have not been enrolling as many students as they did at their peak (Finnigan & Holme, 2015). For example, in St. Louis, Missouri, a regional inter-district plan was created in 1981 as part of a school desegregation lawsuit (*Liddell v. Board of Education of St. Louis*, 1972) that provided students of color in the city of St. Louis the opportunity to attend suburban schools and students in the suburbs could attend magnet schools in the city. At its peak, the program served over 14,000 students and is consistently sought after by families, yet the program is scheduled to be phased out in the 2023–24 school year (Diem & Pinto, 2017; VICC, 2017).

CONCLUSION

As school choice policies continue to gain popularity, it is important for school leaders to have a working knowledge of how they operate and their racial ramifications for schools and communities. We need to ensure that school leaders develop anti-racist mindsets that can challenge the ways that policies like school choice can exacerbate inequality, particularly for marginalized students (Diem et al., 2019). These types of anti-racist identities can be developed in leadership preparation programs but they must continue to be cultivated once leaders assume their roles and throughout the course of their careers.

DISCUSSION QUESTIONS

1. Does a school choice policy exist in your school district? How does the policy account for race and racial diversity?
2. How is school choice perceived in your district? Has your district experienced resistance, pushback, and/or racialized responses to the school choice policy? As a school leader, how would you address and challenge racialized responses to school choice?
3. Are there schools that are more popular and "oversubscribed" in your district? Are these schools racially identifiable? That is, are these schools populated by certain racial groups?
4. How has school choice affected funding in your district and/or state?
5. How are families informed about school choice in your district? Is this information easily accessible to all families?
6. What are the best ways for school choice options (e.g., charter schools, magnet schools) to go about enrolling a racially diverse student population?

SCHOOL CHOICE RESOURCES

- Integrated Schools: https://integratedschools.org/
- Magnet School Assistance Program Center: https://msapcenter.com/
- The National Coalition on School Diversity: https://school-diversity.org/
- National Education Policy Center: https://nepc.colorado.edu/
- School Diversity Notebook: https://sdnotebook.com/
- State Departments of Education (see state websites)
- U.S. Department of Education: www.ed.gov/

NOTE

1 The terms desegregation and integration are often used interchangeably while they have very distinct definitions. Desegregation is "the legal or political process of ending the separation and isolation of different racial and ethnic groups" that "is achieved through court order or voluntary means" (Ayscue & Frankenberg, 2016, n.p.). Integration is "a social process in which members of different racial and ethnic groups experience fair and equal treatment within a desegregated environment" that "requires further action beyond desegregation" (Ayscue & Frankenberg, 2016, n.p.).

RECOMMENDED READINGS

Berends, M., Waddington, J., & Schoenig, J. (Eds.). (2019). *School choice at the crossroads: Research perspectives.* New York: Routledge.

Buras, K. L. (2015). *Charter schools, race, and urban space: Where the market meets grassroots resistance.* New York: Routledge.

Holme, J. J. (2002). Buying homes, buying schools: School choice and the social construction of school quality *Harvard Educational Review, 72*(2), 177–205.

Lareau, A., & Goyette, K. (Eds.). (2014). *Choosing homes, choosing schools.* New York: Russell Sage Foundation.

Mathis, W. J., & Welner, K.G. (2016). *Research-based options for education policymaking: Do choice policies segregate schools?* Boulder, CO: National Education Policy Center.

Miron, G., Welner, J. G., Hinchey, P. H., & Mathis, W. J. (2012). *Exploring the school choice universe: Evidence and recommendations.* Charlotte, NC: Information Age Publishing, Inc.

Orfield, G., & Frankenberg, E. (Eds.). (2013). *Educational delusions? Why choice can deepen inequality and how to make schools fair.* Berkeley, CA: University of California Press.

Roda, A., & Wells, A. S. (2013). School choice policies and racial segregation: Where white parents' good intentions, anxiety, and privilege collide. *American Journal of Education, 119*(2), 261–293.

REFERENCES

Aggarwal, U. (2015). School choice: The freedom to choose, the right to exclude. In B. Picower & E. Mayorga (Eds.), *What's race got to do with it? How current school reform policy maintains racial and economic inequality* (pp. 103–120). New York: Peter Lang.

Anderson, J., & Frankenberg, E. (2019). Voluntary integration in uncertain times. *Phi Delta Kappan, 100*(5), 14–18.

Ayscue, J., & Frankenberg, E. (2016). Desegregation and integration. *Oxford Bibliographies.* DOI: 10.1093/OBO/9780199756810-0139.

Beal, H. K. O., & Hendry, P. M. (2012). The ironies of school choice: Empowering parents and reconceptualizing public education. *American Journal of Education, 118*(4), 521–550.

Berkeley Unified School District. (2019). *Information on Berkeley Unified's Student Assignment Plan.* Retrieved from www.berkeleyschools.net/information-on-berkeley-unifieds-student-assignment-plan/

Billingham, C. M., & Hunt, M. O. (2016). School racial composition and parental choice: New evidence on the preferences of White parents in the United States. *Sociology of Education, 89*(2), 99–117.

Brown v. Board of Education of Topeka, 347 U.S. 483 (1954).

Brown v. Board of Education of Topeka (II), 349 U.S. 294 (1955).

Christensen, B., Eaton, M., Garet, M., Miller, L., Hikowa, H., & DuBois, P. (2003). *Evaluation of the Magnet Schools Assistance Program*. Washington, D.C.: U.S. Department of Education, Office of the Under Secretary.

Clotfelter, C. (2004). *After Brown: The rise and retreat of school desegregation*. Princeton, NJ: Princeton University Press.

Clotfelter, C., Ladd, H., & Vigdor, J. (2010). Teacher mobility, school segregation, and pay-based policies to level the playing field. *Education, Finance, and Policy, 6*(3), 339–438.

Diem, S. (2012). The relationship between policy design, context, and implementation in integration plans. *Education Policy Analysis Archives, 20*(23), 1–39.

Diem, S., Carpenter, B. W., & Lewis-Durham, T. (2019). Preparing anti-racist school leaders in a school choice context. *Urban Education, 54*(5), 706-731.

Diem, S., & Hawkman, A. M. (2019). Whiteness as policy: Reconstructing racial privilege through school choice. In J. S. Brooks & G. Theoharis (Eds.), *Whiteucation: Privilege, power, and prejudice in school and society*. New York: Routledge.

Diem, S., & Pinto, R. (2017). Promoting racial and socioeconomic integration in public schools. *Equity by Design*. Midwest & Plains Equity Assistance Center (MAP EAC).

Feinberg, W., & Lubienski, C. (Eds.). (2008). *School choice policies and outcomes: Empirical and philosophical perspectives*. Albany, NY: State University of New York Press.

Finnigan, K. S., & Holme, J. J. (2015). Regional educational equity policies: Learning from inter district integration programs. Washington, D.C.: *The National Coalition on School Diversity*.

Finnigan, K. S., Holme, J. J., Orfield, M., Luce, T., Diem, S., Mattheis, A., & Hylton, N. D. (2015). Regional educational policy analysis: Rochester, Omaha, and Minneapolis' Inter-district arrangements. *Educational Policy, 29*(5), 780–814.

Frankenberg, E., Anderson, J. & Taylor, K. (2017). *Voluntary integration in U.S. school districts, 2000–2015*. State College, PA: Center for Education and Civil Rights.

Frankenberg, E., & Le, C.Q. (2009). The post-Seattle/Louisville challenge: Extra-legal obstacles to integration. *Ohio State Law Journal, 69*(5), 1015–1072.

Frankenberg, E., & Siegel-Hawley, G. (2008). *The forgotten choice? Rethinking magnet schools in a changing landscape*. Los Angeles, CA: University of California, The Civil Rights Project/Proyecto Derechos Civiles.

Frankenberg, E., Siegel-Hawley, G., & Wang, J. (2011). Choice without equity: Charter school segregation. *Educational Policy Analysis Archives, 19*(1), 1–96.

Fuller, B., Elmore, R. F., & Orfield, G. (Eds.). (1996). *Who chooses? Who loses? Culture, institutions, and the unequal effects of school choice*. New York: Teachers College Press.

Green v. County School Board of New Kent County, 391 U.S. 430 (1968).

Greenblat, A. (2018). Do charter schools worsen segregation? *Governing*. Retrieved from www.governing.com/topics/education/gov-charter-schools-segregation.html

Griffin v. County School Board of Prince Edward County, 377 U.S. 218 (1964).

Grooms, A. A., & Williams, S. M. (2015). The reversed role of magnets in St. Louis: Implications for black student outcomes. *Urban Education, 50*(4), 454–473.

Holme, J. J., Carkhum, R., & Rangel, V. S. (2013). High pressure reform: Examining urban schools' response to multiple school choice policies. *The Urban Review, 45*(2), 167–196.

Holme, J. J., Diem, S., & Welton, A. D. (2014). Suburban school districts and demographic change: The technical, normative, and political dimensions of response. *Educational Administration Quarterly, 50*(1), 34–66.

Holme, J. J., Frankenberg, E., Diem, S., & Welton, A. D. (2013). School choice in suburbia: The impact of choice policies on the potential for suburban integration. *Journal of School Choice: International Research and Reform, 7*(2), 113–141.

Holme, J. J., & Wells, A. S. (2008). School choice beyond district borders: Lessons for the reauthorization of NCLB from interdistrict desegregation and open enrollment plans. In R. Kahlenberg (Ed.), *Improving on No Child Left Behind* (pp. 139–216). New York: The Century Foundation.

Jabbar, H. (2015a). Competitive networks and school leaders' perceptions: The formation of an education marketplace in post-Katrina New Orleans. *American Educational Research Journal, 52*(6), 1093–1131.

Jabbar, H. (2015b). "Every kid is money": Market-like competition and school leader strategies in New Orleans. *Educational Evaluation and Policy Analysis, 37*(4), 638–659.

Jennings, J. (2010). School choice or schools' choice? Managing in an era of accountability. *Sociology of Education, 83*(3), 227–247.

Kahlenberg, R. D. (2016). *School integration in practice: Lessons from nine districts*. New York: The Century Foundation.

Kahlenberg, R. D., & Potter, H. (2014, August 30). The original charter school vision. *The New York Times*. Retrieved from www.nytimes.com/2014/08/31/opinion/sunday/albert-shanker-the-original-charter-school-visionary.html

Meckler, L. (2018, September 4). The education of Betsy DeVos: Why her school choice agenda has not advanced. *The Washington Post*. Retrieved from www.washingtonpost.com/local/education/the-education-of-betsy-devos-why-her-school-choice-agenda-has-crashed/2018/09/04/c21119b8-9666-11e8-810c-5fa705927d54_story.html?utm_term=.f9a62182d928

Mickelson, R. A. (2011). The reciprocal relationship between housing and school integration. Washington, D.C.: *The National Coalition on School Diversity*.

Mills, J. N., & Wolf, P. J. (2017). Vouchers in the Bayou: The effects of the Louisiana scholarship program on student achievement after 2 years. *Educational Evaluation and Policy Analysis, 39*(3), 464–484.

Miron, G., & Welner, K. (2013). Introduction. In G. Miron, K. G. Welner, P. H. Hinchey, & W. J. Mathis. (Eds.), *Exploring the school choice universe: Evidence and recommendations* (pp. 1–16). Charlotte, NC: Information Age Publishing.

Orfield, G. (2013). Choice and civil rights: Forgetting history, facing consequences. In G. Orfield & E. Frankenberg (Eds.), *Educational delusions? Why choice can deepen inequality and how to make schools fair* (pp. 3–35). Berkeley, CA: University of California Press.

Orfield, G., & Eaton, S. E. (1996). *Dismantling desegregation: The quiet reversal of Brown v. Board of Education.* New York: The New Press.

Parents Involved in Community Schools v. Seattle School District No. 1, 551 U.S. 701 (2007).

Potter, H., & Quick, K. (2018). *Diverse-by-design charter schools.* New York: The Century Foundation. Retrieved from https://tcf.org/content/report/diverse-design-charter-schools/

Potter, H., Quick, K., & Davies, E. (2016). *A new wave of school integration.* New York: The Century Foundation.

Quick, K. (2016a). *Hartford Public Schools: Striving for equity through interdistrict programs.* New York: The Century Foundation. Retrieved from https://tcf.org/content/report/hartford-public-schools/

Quick, K. (2016b). *How to achieve socioeconomic integration in schools.* New York: The Century Foundation. Retrieved from https://tcf.org/content/facts/achieve-socioeconomic-integration-schools/

Quick, K. (2018). *City Garden Montessori School: Building an anti-racist community.* New York: The Century Foundation. Retrieved from https://tcf.org/content/report/city-garden-montessori-school/

Reardon, S. F. & Owens, A. (2014). 60 years after Brown: Trends and consequences of school segregation. *Annual Review of Sociology, 40,* 199–214.

Rich, P. M., & Jennings, J. L. (2015). Choice, information, and constrained options: School transfers in a stratified educational system. *American Sociological Review, 80*(5), 1069–1098.

Roda, A., & Wells, A. S. (2013). School choice policies and racial segregation: Where white parents' good intentions, anxiety, and privilege collide. *American Journal of Education, 119*(2), 261–293.

Rothstein, R. (2017). *The color of law: A forgotten history of how our government segregated America.* New York: Liveright Publishing Corporation.

Rumberger. R. W., & Palardy, G. J. (2005). Does segregation still matter? The impact of student composition on academic achievement in high school. *Teachers College Record, 107*(9), 1999–2045.

Saporito, S., & Sohoni, D. (2006). Coloring outside the lines: Racial segregation in public schools and their attendance boundaries. *Sociology of Education, 79*(2), 81–105.

Saporito, S., & Sohoni, D. (2007). Mapping educational inequality: Concentrations of poverty among poor and minority students in public schools. *Social Forces, 85*(3), 1227–1254.

Schneider, M., & Buckley, J. (2002). What do parents want from schools? Evidence from the internet. *Educational Evaluation and Policy Analysis, 24*(2), 133–144.

Scott, J. T. (2005). Introduction: The context of school choice and student diversity. In J. T. Scott (Ed.), *School choice and diversity: What the evidence says* (pp. 1–8). New York: Teachers College Press.

Sheff v. O'Neill, 238 Conn. 1, 678 A.2d 1267 (1996).

Siegel-Hawley, G. (2016). *When the fences come down: Twenty-first century lessons from metropolitan school desegregation*. Chapel Hill, NC: The University of North Carolina Press.

Smrekar, C., & Goldring, E. (1999). *School choice in urban America: Magnet schools and the pursuit of equity*. New York: Teachers College Press.

Smrekar, C., & Honey, N. (2015). The desegregation aims and demographic contexts of magnet schools: How parents choose and why siting policies matter. *Peabody Journal of Education, 90*(1), 128–55.

Strauss, V. (2014, May 20). A dozen problems with charter schools. *The Washington Post*. Retrieved from www.washingtonpost.com/news/answer-sheet/wp/2014/05/20/a-dozen-problems-with-charter-schools/?utm_term=.9959692cc394

Strauss, V. (2016, October 21). Obama's real education legacy: Common core, testing, charter schools. *The Washington Post*. Retrieved from www.washingtonpost.com/news/answer-sheet/wp/2016/10/21/obamas-real-education-legacy-common-core-testing-charter-schools/

Swann v. Charlotte-Mecklenburg Board of Education, 402 U.S. 1 (1971).

Turner, E. O. (2018). Marketing diversity: Selling school districts in a racialized marketplace. *Journal of Education Policy, 33*(6), 793–817.

Voluntary Interdistrict Choice Corporation (VICC). (2017). *Answers to frequently asked questions (FAQ)*. Retrieved from http://www/choicecorp.org/

Waddington, R. J., & Berends, M. (2018). Impact of the Indiana choice scholarship program: Achievement affects for students in upper elementary and middle school. *Journal of Policy Analysis and Management, 37*(4), 783–808.

Wells, A. S. (2014). *Seeing past the "colorblind" myth: Why education policymakers should address racial and ethnic inequality and support culturally diverse schools*. Boulder, CO: National Education Policy Center.

Wells, A. S., Baldridge, B. J., Duran, J., Grzesikowski, C., Lofton, R., Roda, A., Warner, M., & White, T. (2009). *Boundary crossing for diversity, equity and achievement: Inter-district school desegregation and educational opportunity*. Cambridge, MA: Charles Hamilton Houston Institute for Race and Justice at Harvard Law School.

Welner, K. G. (2006). K-12 race-conscious student assignment policies: Law, social science, and diversity. *Review of Educational Research, 76*(3), 349–382.

White, T. (2015). Charter schools: demystifying whiteness in a market of "no excuses" corporate-styled charter schools. In B. Picower & E. Mayorga (Eds.), *What's race got to do with it? How current school reform policy maintains racial and economic inequality* (pp. 121–146). New York: Peter Lang.

Zimmer, A. (2018). *Blackstone Valley Prep: Intentionally diverse network with strong college prep focus*. New York: The Century Foundation. Retrieved from https://tcf.org/content/report/blackstone-valley-prep/

Chapter 4

The Racial Politics of School Closure and Community Response

Over the last decade, school closure has become one of the most publicly contested and emotionally embroiled reforms, with numerous examples in both the media and scholarly discourse of how policy and school district officials are at odds with teachers' unions, students and families, and even grassroots community organizers over the imminent closure of neighborhood schools and the long-term impact it would have on the surrounding community (Diem & Welton, 2017; Lipman, 2011; Stovall, 2013; Welton & Freelon, 2018). Proponents view school closure as a possible fresh start for students and families in schools that are chronically struggling. They also consider it the most expedient solution to a number of district concerns such as declining student enrollment, repeated poor academic performance, budget limitations, and competition from other school choices such as private schools, charters, magnet programs, and selective public schools (Diem & Welton, 2017; Kirshner & Gaertner, 2015; Siegel-Hawley, Bridges, & Shields, 2017).

Irrespective of the reasons policy makers and district administration give for closing a school, in most cases the impact the final policy decision will have on students, families of color, and their neighborhoods ultimately is not the priority. Therefore, we find the typical justifications for school closure to be racialized as they focus on the bottom-line instead of examining the full complexity of the issues at hand, especially how high stakes school closure is for communities of color. This is in part why opponents of school closure and related market-driven reforms—namely, teachers, parents, and grassroots community organizers—continue to argue that the underlying intentions behind the reform strategy are in fact racist, and part of a larger scheme to gentrify low-income and working-class Black and Latinx neighborhoods to then monopolize the market with school choice and privatization (Diem & Welton, 2017; Johnson, 2012; Journey 4 Justice Alliance, 2014; Kirshner & Pozzoboni, 2011).

Although the political battle over school closure is more likely to get played out amongst stakeholders at the local level, the policy's origins are indeed federal. Previously, under the No Child Left Behind Act (NCLB) of 2001, led by the Bush Administration, when a Title I school failed to achieve Adequate Yearly Progress (AYP) for five consecutive years school districts were mandated to then initiate plans for restructuring by either closing the school and re-opening it as a charter, replacing all or most of the school personnel, or seeking out a private entity to manage the operations of the school (U.S. DOE, 2003). Later, the Obama Administration followed suit in 2009 by increasing federal funding for and expanding the scope of the School Improvement Grant (SIG) program, an initiative formerly established under NCLB (Trujillo & Renée, 2012). The SIG program aimed to "turnaround" the nation's lowest-performing schools by requiring recipients to choose among four intervention models, and the first three models—turnaround, transformation, and restart—were similar to the corrective action provisions under NCLB. However, the Obama Administration took the already punitive nature of the SIG program a step further by adding complete closure of a school as the fourth option. Thus, school closure, like school choice, is by no means a partisan issue: both Democrat and Republican political leaders have endorsed the neoliberal principles underlying the educational reform (see Pew, 2011). In essence, the federal government has played a major role in creating a gateway for the private sector to gain a foothold in public education and benefit from widespread closure of public schools.

Though federal policies like NCLB set the national blueprint for school closure, the localized politics of school closures in urban, suburban, and even rural communities across the country all have one commonality—Black and Latinx students and families are most negatively impacted by the reform. For example, one of the most widely publicized series of mass school closures, which occurred in Chicago Public Schools (CPS), closed, turned around, or consolidated over 100 schools prior to 2013 (Diem & Welton, 2017). Then, in 2013, the mayoral-appointed Board of Education voted to close another 50 schools, all predominately in Black and Latinx communities, representing at that point in time the largest single sweep of school closures to occur in U.S. history (Lipman, Vaughan, & Gutierrez, 2014). Very few urban school districts across the country are immune to school closure as Black and Latinx students and families in Philadelphia, Detroit, St. Louis, Kansas City, Oakland, Houston, New Orleans, and numerous other cities continue to endure aftershocks of the reform.

One major color-evasive assumption of school closure policies is that once a school is closed its students will be able to move onto higher quality schooling options. Yet, school closure does quite the opposite, as research suggests most students affected by school closure relocate to an equal to or lower-performing school, thus experiencing little to no academic improvement (Barnum, 2019). Moreover, when a school is closed it disrupts its local community, depleting it of resources, especially young people's social capital or valuable ties to their local community (Kirshner & Pozzoboni, 2011). Stakeholders most affected by school closure, such as students, families, and teachers, are more than often left out of the decision-making process when their neighborhood school is slated to be closed (Stovall, 2013; Welton & Freelon, 2018).

However, there are a number of grassroots activists of color that are leading the charge in interrogating school closure policies by offering more effective policy alternatives we consider to be anti-racist. Subsequently in this chapter we provide examples of ways in which local school parents and community activists across the country are organizing to keep their schools open, and how district and school administrators can learn from communities of color's efforts to redress racial inequities in their neighborhood schools. Following an analysis of the number of color-evasive rationales educational administrators, policy makers, and even some researchers give for disproportionately closing schools in low-income, Black, and Latinx neighborhoods, we provide strategies for how educational leadership, when approached through the lens of anti-racism, can be a collective effort among administrators, parents, teachers, and students fighting to put an end to school closure.

THE COLOR-EVASIVE, MARKET-BASED AGENDA BEHIND SCHOOL CLOSURES

Typically, the justifications policy makers and district officials give for closing schools are either declining student enrollment, budget shortfalls, building underutilization, and/or persistent low academic performance (Pew, 2011). For instance, Chicago Public Schools' (CPS) policy outlined three explanations for closing schools: (1) *non-academic*: space underutilization, poor building infrastructure, other competing priorities for building use, or converting the school to a charter; (2) *academic*: a failure to demonstrate academic improvement after being placed on probation; or (3) *a change in educational focus*: a re-orientation that may radically alter the curriculum and instructional programs for faculty and students (de la Torre & Gwynne, 2009). According to de la Torre and Gwynne's (2009) study of school closure in CPS most schools were closed for either space underutilization or academic reasons.

Still, the problems anticipated to be resolved by school closure can still go unresolved. For example, the Pew Charitable Trust (2011) found in its study of large city district budgets that little money was saved from closing schools, and the only savings obtained were when school districts coupled school closures with substantial layoffs. In the six districts studied in the foundation's report, the annual savings were less than $1 million per school closed. The process of closing a school came with additional unanticipated price tags such as

> expenses associated with mothballing and maintaining sites; transitioning students; moving desks, computers and other district property; and making improvements to the remaining schools, particularly those receiving displaced students.
>
> (p. 6)

Also, in terms of building underutilization, Pew found the urban districts that it studied procured hardly any, if at all, profit from the sale or leasing of school buildings due to their old age and poor condition.

In urban contexts there is a well-documented pattern of how the mass closure of schools creates a window of opportunity for the private market, including charter schools, voucher programs, and even state takeover (Good, 2016; Lipman, 2011). The national network of grassroots community, youth, and parent-led organizations, Journey for Justice (J4J, 2014), calls this mass closure of public schools in urban communities across the country an "epidemic" that is shrinking public school districts while, inversely, rapidly expanding the number of charter schools through the repeated "downward spiral" of events. First, underfunding and criticism of public schools pushes families away. Next, parents may seek out new charter schools, especially those promoted by the media and policy makers. Then, conditions decline in both public schools and their surrounding communities as they continue to receive fewer and fewer resources while serving higher-needs students. These deteriorating conditions in public schools also push away good teachers. Subsequently, schools that are labeled as "failing" or "underutilized" are closed. These initial closures then lead to additional attacks on public schools, more budget cuts, more deterioration of public schools and surrounding communities, and more quality teachers and families leaving (J4J, 2014). J4J underscores that it is up to policy makers to end this pattern by intervening and advocating *for* public schools.

As urban school districts continue to permanently close schools in mass numbers, there is fertile ground for charter school expansion. While we can't address all cases of how charter expansion adversely prompted the closure of public schools in detail, we do highlight a noted few. In 2002 the State of Pennsylvania took over the Philadelphia public school system to resolve the district's financial insolvency, a decision led by both a Republican governor and state legislature. The first 10 years of state takeover coincided with an increase in charter school student enrollment from 16,000 to 50,000, and a 25% drop in enrollment for schools still managed by the school district (Good, 2016). Subsequently, in 2012 the continued decline in student enrollment and fiscal debt, plus additional state funding cuts, prompted closure of one-sixth of Philadelphia's schools still operated by the district (Good, 2016).

Similarly, Detroit Public Schools, under state emergency financial management (i.e., state takeover), faced a budget deficit of 30%, in addition to a 63% decline in student enrollment between 2005–2013 (Pew, 2011). As a result, well over 200 public schools in Detroit have closed since 2000, whereas charter school enrollment increased 63% between 2005–2013 (J4J, 2014). The school district's extreme drop in student enrollment coincided with the city's significant population decline. Detroit, a city where 81% of the residents are Black, between 1980 and 2014 lost approximately 500,000 residents (42%) and experienced its largest population decline between 2000 and 2014 with a loss of 255,000 residents (Pizarek, Rubin, & Schildt, 2017). At its peak in 1950, Detroit had a population of 1.5 million; it has now been reduced to approximately 670,000 residents. While a number of social, political, and economic issues contributed to Detroit's population decline, the most noted was in 2013 when Detroit became the largest American city to file for bankruptcy (Davey & Walsh, 2013).

But it is New Orleans that represents the most unprecedented citywide occupation of charters, where in the aftermath of Hurricane

Katrina in 2005 the state-run Louisiana Recovery School District (RSD) fired 7,000 public school teachers and since 2003 has closed and reopened every public school as a charter, with the exception of five (Brown, 2015; J4J, 2014). Now RSD is the first 100% charter school district in the country. One commonality across Philadelphia, Detroit, and New Orleans is that the charter market took advantage of each city and its public-school district's series of hardships to gain entry into the educational marketplace. Hence, privatization capitalized off of the distress of these urban cities and their school districts, and by default the families and students of color they mostly serve.

We recognize that any policy decision district administrators must make to protect the learning and well-being of all students as well as the interest of all communities in the district is no small task. Nevertheless, we still view policy makers and district officials' justifications for school closure to be shortsighted [race-neutral] practicalities that fail to examine the full-picture of how and why the circumstances leading up to a school(s) being cast as "failing" or too much of a challenge to "save" perhaps transpired in the first place. Thus far, in all cases nationwide the decision to close schools has disproportionately not been in the best interests of low-income, students of color and families. There are a host of other complex problems tied to the "reasons" for school closure that continue to be ignored or not considered, like ongoing residential racial segregation/isolation linked to a history of housing discrimination and limited employment opportunities, commerce, and overall economic depletion in Black communities that unfortunately is still largely government sanctioned (see Anderson, 2016, pp. 115–116; Rothstein, 2017). Rather, in most cases, as we will discuss further, policy makers and district leaders' decision to close schools is both a hasty and temporary remedy, that still does not address the underlying issues of institutional and structural racism and inequities that remain.

RACIAL REPERCUSSIONS: WHO BEARS THE BURDEN OF SCHOOL CLOSURES?

Policy makers and district officials in most cases during the policy decision-making process have given limited consideration of *who* will be disparately impacted by school closures. The disproportionate impact of school closure in the U.S. by race is not just an urban phenomenon, but also an issue in suburban and rural contexts as well (Gallagher & Gold, 2017). A research study from the Urban Institute found that between the 2012–2013 and 2013–2014 school years, nationally Black students represented 31% of students in urban schools that remained open but disproportionally accounted for 61% of students in schools that were permanently closed; white students, however, represented 19% of students in the schools that remained open and only 7% of students in schools that were closed. In suburban districts Black students represented 29% of students in schools that were closed, which outweighed their representation of students (14%) in schools that remained open. Comparatively, white suburban students were underrepresented in their proportion of students in closed schools at 43%, when compared to their proportion (54%) of students in suburban schools that remained open. Finally, though white students represent the majority in rural school districts, Latinx students in comparison were still slightly overrepresented in schools that closed at 14% compared to their representation of students, almost 12%, in rural schools that remained open (Gallagher & Gold, 2017).

Although, the national discourse on school closures centers primarily on urban contexts, this same study from the Urban Institute counters this assumption with findings that suggest most school closures occur in suburban school districts. For example, in 2012–13, 53% of school closures were in suburban areas, 26% in rural, with slightly less school closures, 21%, in urban areas (Gallagher & Gold, 2017).

However, in urban areas there is a distinctive geography of race in terms of how school closure plays out, as it is an intersection of where someone lives and their racial background that unfortunately determines the probability of impact by school closure. One prime example is Chicago, where politicians and district officials presented their decision-making criteria for school closure as not being about race per se (i.e., race-neutral), but rather consisting of other factors like enrollment decline, low performance, and space underutilization. Yet, the effects of school closure are indeed racist. Black students, who represent 40% of the student population in CPS, but 88% of the students affected by school closure, disproportionately are the largest racial group impacted by school closures in Chicago (OTL, 2013). Latinx students, the largest racial/ethnic subgroup, represent 10% of students affected by school closure, and white students less than 1%. Then, when geography is coupled with race what is revealed is that the majority of schools closed are located in zip codes comprised of majority Black and low-income populations, as well as those schools located in zip codes on the South Side of the city (Johnson, 2012).

In our own research, we examined linkages between the geography of race and school closures in Chicago (Diem & Welton, 2017). In Figure 4.1 we provide a map of Chicago that substantiates the severity with which certain racial subgroups experience school closure. In the map, the dark grey areas represent a higher percentage of white students, medium grey areas for Black students, light grey for Latinx students, and white for Asian students. Each dot signifies a school that was closed, and is color-coded to represent the policy timeline in which the school was closed. Light grey dot schools were closed as a result of Renaissance 2010, which was a massive school restructuring policy led by then chief of schools Arne Duncan to radically alter public education in Chicago and introduce market-based approaches. Sixty schools were closed as a result of this policy. Medium grey dots represent the additional 50 schools closed in 2013 by the Board of Education appointed by Mayor Rahm Emanuel. Finally, black dots represent charter schools situated in the area. We will discuss later in this chapter the role school district leaders and city officials played in spearheading school closure policies. Hence, this map illustrates the geography of race and school closures, substantiating the notion that predominately Black communities are most affected by school closures.

Similarly, Lee and Lubienski (2017), using Geographic Information System data, created cartograms to investigate the level of equitable access to schooling after the mass school closures of 2013 in Chicago. While school closures caused moderate inequity in access for most students, the researchers found that in areas with a high density of African American and Latinx children aged 5 to 14 there is a negative change in access to schooling after school closures. Even more specifically, neighborhoods with a high cluster of African American children presented a small but significant difference in accessibility to schooling after closures. The researchers also considered the intersection of race and specific neighborhood location and found that African American children living in southern areas of Chicago experience a moderate change in access to schooling, whereas children in northern areas experience a significant increase in travel time and distance after school closings. School closure also affects other vulnerable populations. For instance, in 2013 homeless students represented 8% (2,615) of the 31,438 students affected by school closure in Chicago (Chicago Coalition for the Homeless, 2013).

There is also concern that students displaced by school closure will have to cross gang territories and risk violence en route to their new school (J4J, 2014), and Lee & Lubienski's (2017) research corroborates

66 THE RACIAL POLITICS OF SCHOOL CLOSURE

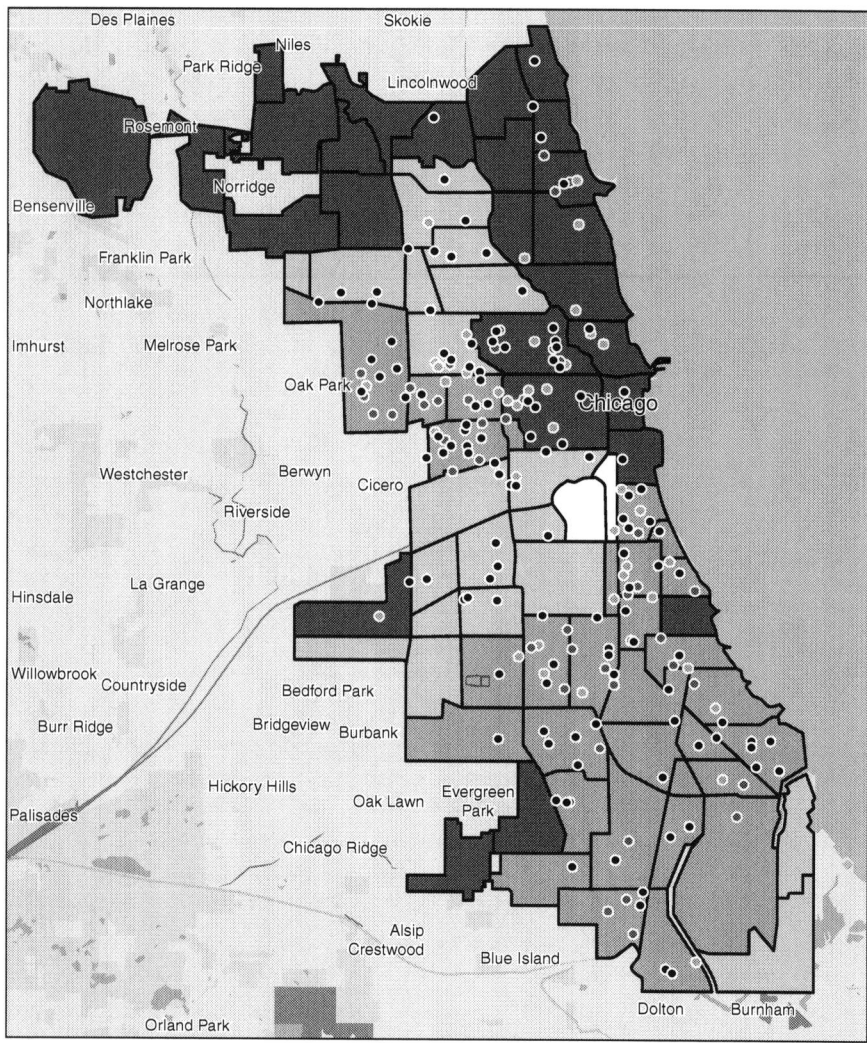

Figure 4.1 Chicago community areas by race and type of school closure
Source: Diem and Welton (2017).

this concern. They found that children living in areas of higher incidence of dangerous and unhealthy factors (e.g., gang activity, vacant buildings, graffiti, crime) experience the most significant inequities in access to schooling after closure, and are more likely to travel to school through areas with high incidence of crime. In response to community concern about student safety post school closures, CPS initiated the Safe

Passage program to provide community escorts who protect students while traveling to their new school, but critics argue this program is not enough to safeguard students from gang violence (Ahmed-Ullah, 2013). Based on their findings, Lee and Lubienski (2017) conclude that the school closure policy not only exacerbates racial inequities in access to quality schooling but also reinforces racial segregation in Chicago.

> CPS school closing policy—based on the capacity and the number of empty seats at schools—raised the likelihood that students in segregated, geographically discontinuous communities had less access to neighboring schools within the commutable travel time. In other words, the school closings bring educational inequality to predominately disadvantaged neighborhoods, which in turn exacerbates segregation and inequality in metropolitan areas.
> (Lee & Lubienski, 2017, p. 70)

Similar to Chicago, the 2013 school closures in Philadelphia precipitated a pattern of racial and geographic inequities. That year 81% of African American students were impacted by school closures, yet they represented just 58% of the total student population, an evident disproportionality (Schott Foundation, 2013). In terms of geographic location, most of the school closures occurred in African American neighborhoods in Lower North Philadelphia and West Philadelphia. Unfortunately, school closure was just another disparity to add to the long history of "discriminatory investments and disinvestments" from predominately African American neighborhoods in Philadelphia (Good, 2016, p. 879). The disproportionate effect of school closures on Black and Brown neighborhoods extends beyond educational inequities. In communities of color, the neighborhood school is often a symbol of the community's cultural history, and closing the school not only erases a community's sense of identity but also the community ties that are a deeply important form of social and cultural capital (see Cobb, 2015; Johnson, 2012).

In addition, the Collaborative for Equity and Justice in Education (2014) at the University of Illinois, Chicago found that school closures in Chicago adversely affect parent involvement. Parents and caregivers reported that prior to closure they were deeply involved in their schools and filled many needed roles such as volunteer coaches, classroom aides, and community liaisons. In the Collaborative's study several parents reported that they felt excluded, unwelcomed, and that they were not encouraged to be as involved in their new school. Moreover, parents felt CPS did not listen to their concerns about the decision to close their school, and as a result they had a growing mistrust of the district.

POLITICIANS = COLOR-EVASIVE EDUCATIONAL LEADERSHIP

Typically, in the case of school closures it is not school administrators with years of training and preparation to lead schools who have the most power to make key leadership decisions, but in fact politicians. Urban school districts are often taken over by the state or subject to mayoral control because policy makers aim to fix what they believe traditional school leadership has been unable to. Mayoral and state regimes have yet to live up to their promises of instant academic gains or financial recovery, but instead have managed to radically alter the urban public school landscape by shutting tax payers out of public school decision-making and leaving low-income, working class communities of color with little to no public neighborhood schooling options (see Pew, 2016).

Currently, there are 15 mayoral-controlled school districts in the U.S., and this governance structure typically limits local school community voice, and unfortunately for this reason is an opportune space for policies like school closures (Pew, 2016). Mayoral-controlled districts are managed using more corporatized structures where traditionally elected boards are replaced with a mayoral-appointed board. Also, under a mayoral-controlled structure the superintendent position, typically held by a certified and seasoned career educational administrator, who has been rigorously vetted, is replaced by and rebranded as a mayoral-appointed Chief Executive Officer (CEO) or Chancellor. In many cases appointed CEOs or Chancellors have limited prior experience in the education field, and some are even recruited from the corporate world or held other prior political positions. Even when a CEO/Chancellor does have some previous experience in education, they often have ties to foundations and organizations with neoliberal agendas, and brand themselves as educational "reformers" who have what it takes to rapidly execute policies and decisions that are usually steeped in the ideology of the market, and that they firmly believe will clean up what the public has deemed to be a broken school system. This type of unilateral organizational arrangement permits hasty approval and execution of widespread neoliberal educational reforms because there is no public input or approval, and so the educational policy processes under mayoral control are grossly anti-democratic.

One of the most controversial mayoral-appointed public school figures is former Chancellor of D.C. Public Schools Michelle Rhee, who resigned in 2010 after voters adamantly chose not to reelect her boss Mayor Adrian Fenty. Voters were disgruntled over a number of Rhee's polarizing educational reforms—like closing two dozen schools—that Mayor Fenty gave her carte blanche to implement without community input (Hopkinson, 2010; Mead, 2017; Strauss, 2017). Another polemic educational reformer, former Secretary of Education Arne Duncan, when serving as CEO of Chicago Public Schools under Mayor Richard M. Daley, on September 22, 2004 unveiled Renaissance 2010, which is a policy that forever changed the landscape of CPS to a "public" school system that is now dominated by privatization. The goal of the policy was to close 60 of the district's worst-performing schools, the majority of which were located in Black neighborhoods, and replace them with 100 new schools (mostly charter schools) that were to be held to higher standards of accountability (CPS, 2016). Those supporting Renaissance 2010 gave the usual rationales for school closure like increased academic achievement and opening up more school choice to families via charters. However, opponents felt that the policy simply furthered gentrification, created an open door for privatization in public education, decreased community participation in schools, and subsequently severely disadvantage low-income Black students whose neighborhood schools were mostly likely to be placed on the chopping block as chronically failing (Lipman & Hursh, 2007). Subsequently, as we know, Duncan then replicated his Chicago educational policy platform, an agenda largely backed by corporate entities, at a national scale during his tenure as Secretary of Education in the Obama Administration (Carpenter, 2015).

In our final example of mayoral control, New York City Public Schools, the consequences of mass public school closure are not unlike other high-profile cases where political officials celebrate in the media the immediate improvement in student achievement due to the policy decisions, but the residual racial disparities go unresolved and relatively unmentioned. Former Mayor Bloomberg, along with school district Chancellor Klein, launched a series of interrelated reforms that involved closing over 40 high schools between 2000 and 2014, opening more than 200 new, small, themed high schools, and a school choice program accessible to all students in the district (Kemple, 2015). The politicians anticipated that eliminating high schools with high dropout rates, i.e., "dropout factories", would increase graduation rates and provide more schooling options for students typically assigned to low-performing schools based on where they lived (Kemple, 2015). There were immediate signs of improvement, as students displaced once their high school was closed did transfer to higher-performing schools (Kemple, 2015). Also, students who entered high school post the school closure reform had higher attendance, on-track rates, higher graduation rates, and were more likely to obtain the more rigorous Regents diploma when compared to those who entered high school before the reform.

Unfortunately, though, the improvement post-school closure in NYC Public Schools was short-term. Although students displaced by closure did better at their new school, it was not by much. In the end, only 56% of these students actually graduated from high school, and there were a significant number of students "being left behind" post the implementation of school closures (Kemple, 2015, p. 52). Overall, only 30% of New York City's high school students graduate in four years, and this statistic is worse for Black and Latinx males, of whom only slightly over 50% graduate at all (Kemple, 2015).

COLOR-EVASIVE RESEARCH: LIMITED AND INCONCLUSIVE EVIDENCE ON SCHOOL CLOSURES

School closure is now a widely implemented policy response to chronic school failure in districts primarily serving low-income students of color. Yet ironically, there are very few studies to drawn upon that propose positive outcomes of the reform. There are a few studies with findings suggesting that students displaced by closure who then transfer to academically higher-performing schools show some academic gains. Yet, these findings should be considered with caution, because improvement in academic achievement can only occur *if* a displaced student has the *opportunity* to transfer to a school that is higher performing than the school they left (Engberg, Gill, Zamaro, & Zimmer, 2012). However, most students displaced by closure do not get that opportunity. For instance, Kirshner, Gaertner, and Pozzoboni (2010) found that post-school closure Latinx and African American students in their new school experienced decline in academic performance, were more likely to drop out of school, and less likely to graduate. Finally, students do not necessarily experience the fresh start that is assumed to come with school closure.

Likewise, de la Torre and Gwynne (2009) found in their study of school closures in CPS between 2001 and 2006, that most displaced students re-enrolled in schools that were some of the weakest schools in the school system academically. More specifically, 40% of students displaced re-enrolled in schools that were on probation, and 42% of this same group of students re-enrolled in schools in the bottom quartile of the district on the standardized assessment. At the same time, only 6% transferred to schools that were in the top-quartile in academic performance. The researchers speculate that very few displaced students re-enrolled in top performing schools because limited seats were available, the schools were perhaps too long a distance away to travel, or parents were unfamiliar with the schools' neighborhoods. Moreover, while Reading scores of students displaced by school closure in Chicago got back on track within a year, the Math scores of this same group of students continued to trail behind, and this academic decline is attributed to the disruption that students and their families experienced when transitioning to their new school (Gordon, de la Torre, Cowhy, Moore, Sartain, & Knight, 2018)

We also find that most quantitative research studies on school closure, that is the few that are available, are rather decontextualized and race-neutral in their execution and overall presentation of the findings. These studies for the most part do recognize that school closure is a very controversial and political policy, given there is much public concern for how school closure will impact students, parents, and teachers. Yet, what is pointedly absent from the policy background description in these studies is how the political tensions around school closure are also tied to racial matters, especially the racial realities that school communities threatened by closure face. When discussions of how school closure impacts students of color are generally absent, technical aspects of the policy background, such as the criteria a district or state used to close schools, are provided instead. Furthermore, most quantitative studies on school closure fail to mention any racial indicators or any other intersecting demographic characteristics of the context of study, and when they do, no connections are made between the racial demographics and the policy in question or the study's ultimate findings. For example, Engberg et al. (2012), one of the most widely cited quantitative studies on school closure, did conduct an analysis of the demographic characteristics in the anonymous district they studied, to find that African American students, 48%, and students who receive free and reduced lunch, 84%, were more likely to be displaced by school closure. However, to us the rate at which African American and low-income students experience school closure is disconcerting, given these subpopulations only represented 28% and 69% respectively of the district, a disproportionality that the authors failed to even mention. What's more, the authors did not disaggregate the achievement data of students displaced due to school closure by race.

Nonetheless, the sequence of events surrounding school closure are indeed contextual and, in most cases, localized. For instance, public housing closures in Black neighborhoods across the South Side of Chicago triggered a perpetual decline in student enrollment and subsequent closure of public schools in these communities. The devastation of Hurricane Katrina in New Orleans presented the state with a window of opportunity to unravel and replace the public school system with charters. Then, in Detroit, the series of school closures over time was uniquely tied to the city's financial bankruptcy. These examples represent just a few of the many cases from which to infer that context matters to the nature of school closures.

Two of the most referenced studies in school closure research present what we question as giving too much of a bird's eye view of a policy that has proven to be so locally embroiled. Carlson and Lavertu's (2015) study (supported by Fordham Institute, an organization noted as supporting market-oriented policies), examined school closures in eight major urban public districts in Ohio and charters near these districts; while Brummet (2014) studied elementary and middle school closures in urban and suburban districts in Michigan. Both studies found that displaced students did eventually experience gains in academic achievement at their new school, only if, of course, the new school was higher-achieving than their former one. We have concerns that such a decontextualized, wide lens of analysis at the state level might misleadingly present school closure as a one-size-fits-all policy solution, not taking into account that when it comes to school closure the unique localized context does indeed matter.

RECOMMENDATIONS FOR ANTI-RACIST LEADERSHIP AND POLICYMAKING: TAKING THE LEAD FROM COMMUNITY ORGANIZERS AND ACTIVISTS

There are sites of possibility and hope across the country where community leadership and activism is disrupting the neoliberal agendas of school closure, and also re-imagining schools as a space *for* the community. School community organizing and activism typically involves youth, public school parents, and community members leveraging their collective power to disrupt structures and policies that continue to underserve and deplete their schools and communities of resources and opportunities (Mediratta, Shah, & McAlister, 2008; Renée & McAlister, 2011; Welton & Freelon, 2018). We recommend that policy makers and school administrators take the lead from teachers, as well as students and parents of color in urban schools across the country who are engaging in anti-racist policymaking by using community organizing tools and practices.

One example is Reagan High School (RHS) in Austin, Texas, a school that had significantly declining student enrollment and low academic performance, and in 2009 was given an ultimatum by the state education agency to radically improve in a year or face closure (Brick, 2012). The school remained open due to the collective leadership efforts of the principal, committed teachers, and local community organizers who reimagined how to build an optimal learning environment for the success of young people in their community. Also, a community-based organization, Austin Voices for Education and Youth (AVEY) advocated for RHS to adopt a Community School model, where the school serves as a community hub of social and health services and other community supports (AVEY, 2016). RHS also adopted an Early College model that gives students more opportunities to graduate high school with college credit. Through shared leadership with the principal and community stakeholders who used assets-based approaches as a school reform alternative to punitive actions like schools closure, the high school's graduation rate has doubled (Texas AFT, 2015). Terrance Green's research also emphasizes the importance of community leadership to school reform in urban school communities. Similar to the work of community leaders at RHS, Green (2015) demonstrates how even after a community has experienced the loss of its school closing, with community leadership, voice, and input a high school can be re-opened and reimagined as a Community School. We see the *school as the community nucleus* approach to reform, unlike school closure, as asset-based and even an anti-racist approach that recognizes the community indeed has vital leadership and knowledge to offer the school (Green 2015).

In contrast, communities of color in Chicago have had to navigate the complicated neoliberal undercurrents and racial politics of the urban context, and to get the attention of policy makers in this political climate communities of color have had to engage in more extreme forms of activism. Stovall (2016) who is known for his ongoing scholar-activism and engagement with the Little Village and

North Lawndale communities in Chicago, has written extensively about how these communities came together for a three-week hunger strike to protest the desperate need for a new neighborhood high school. Another example that received national attention was Dyett High School in the South Side Chicago Bronzeville neighborhood, which was one of the 50 schools scheduled to close. In protest to the possibility of school closure, parents, teachers, and other community members staged a 34-day hunger strike, that resulted in the hospitalization of several protestors (Fitzpartrick, 2015). Although the school remained opened in the end, the parent organizers' felt that their voices were not taken seriously by the mayor and other school district officials. For instance, even after their organizing efforts the parent strikers were left out of planning discussions for re-opening the school (Masterson, 2016). The community members, as part of a district-initiated request for proposals (RFP), submitted a proposal to the district to re-open the school as a global leadership and green technology academy. Then at a press conference CPS announced it would re-open Dyett High as an arts-focused school instead, and parent strikers reported they were barred from entering this press conference (Ewing, 2015).

We have provided examples of the hopes and possibilities, but also the realities of the perils communities of color must endure when navigating the neoliberal agendas and racial politics of their schools and districts. Examples of parents-of-color activism like that in Chicago are what David Stovall (2016) calls a necessary interruption to erupt and disrupt racist business-as-usual practices of schooling and policymaking. But we do find it troubling the lengths that communities of color had to go to just to be heard and possibly get a seat at the policymaking table. Therefore, the problem does not lie with the communities of color who are engaging in heroic forms of activism, but with the district officials and policy makers who fail to truly listen.

DISCUSSION QUESTIONS

1. How have school closures, if at all, impacted your community? What are the rationales given for school closures? In your community who is impacted the most by school closures and why?
2. What are some alternative policy solutions to school closure that your community could consider that would be more equity- and justice-oriented?

3. Do communities of color have a voice in school policy and decision-making in your school community? If so, how are these communities engaging in community organizing practices to support equity and justice in schools?
4. Does your school community view communities of color as educational leaders and engage in shared leadership with communities of color? If so, how, and if not, how could you develop spaces for shared leadership with minoritized communities?

SCHOOL CLOSURE RESOURCES

- Collaborative for Equity and Justice in Education: https://ceje.uic.edu/
- Interview with Dr. Eve Ewing author of *Ghosts in the Schoolyard* (2018): www.cc.com/video-clips/va29l1/the-daily-show-with-trevor-noah-eve-l-ewing—breaking-down-structural-racism-with–ghosts-in-the-schoolyard-
- Journey for Justice Alliance: https://j4jalliance.com/
- Schott Foundation for Public Education: http://schottfoundation.org/

RECOMMENDED READINGS

Ewing, E. L. (2018). *Ghosts in the schoolyard: Racism and school closings on Chicago's South Side.* Chicago, IL: University of Chicago Press.

Stovall, D. O. (2016). *Born out of struggle: Critical race theory, school creation, and the politics of interruption.* Albany, NY: SUNY Press.

REFERENCES

Ahmed-Ullah, N. S. (2013, July 17). Gang expert testifies school closures will put kids "in line of fire." *Chicago Tribune.* Retrieved from https://www.chicagotribune.com/news/ct-xpm-2013-07-17-ct-met-cps-closings-hearings-20130717-story.html

Anderson, C. (2016). *White rage: The unspoken truth of our racial divide.* New York: Bloomsbury.

Austin Voices for Education and Youth. (2016). *Reagan community school project.* Austin, TX: Authors. Retrieved from http://austinvoices.org/programs/reagan-community-school-project/

Barnum, M. (February 5, 2019). Five things we've learned from a decade of research on school closures. *Chalkbeat*. Retrieved from www.chalkbeat.org/posts/us/2019/02/05/school-closure-research-review/

Brick, M. (2012). *Saving the school: The true story of a principal, a teacher, a coach, a bunch of kids, and a year in the crosshairs of education reform.* New York: Penguin Press.

Brummet, Q. (2014). The effect of school closings on student achievement. *Journal of Public Economics, 119,* 108–124.

Carlson, D. & Lavertu, S. (2015). *School closures on student achievement: An analysis of Ohio's urban district and charter schools.* Columbus, OH: Thomas B. Fordham Institute. Retrieved from file:///Users/diems/Downloads/School-Closures-and-Student-Achievement-Report-website-final.pdf

Carpenter, Z. (2015, October 12). The legacy of Arne Duncan, 'a hero in the education business.' *The Nation*. Retrieved from https://www.thenation.com/article/archive/the-legacy-of-arne-duncan/

Chicago Coalition for the Homeless. (2013). *Homeless children are 8% of 31,438 students impacted by Chicago Public Schools' closing/merger plans.* Chicago, IL: Authors. Retrieved from www.chicagohomeless.org/cpsclosures/

Chicago Public Schools. (2016). *Renaissance 2010.* Retrieved from www.cps.edu/PROGRAMS/DISTRICTINITIATIVES/Pages/Renaissance2010.asxpx

Cobb, J. (2015). The life and death of Jamaica High School. *The New Yorker*. Retrieved from www.newyorker.com/magazine/2015/08/31/class-notes-annals-of-education-jelanicobb

The Collaborative for Equity and Justice in Education. (2014). *The impact of school closings on parent involvement.* Chicago, IL: College of Education, University of Illinois at Chicago. Retrieved from https://ceje.uic.edu/wp-content/uploads/2013/11/CEJE-%20parent-participation-2014.02.22.pdf

Davey, M., & Walsh, M. W. (2013, July 18). Billions in debt, Detroit tumbles into insolvency. *The New York Times*. Retrieved from www.nytimes.com/2013/07/19/us/detroit-files-for-bankruptcy.html

de la Torre, M., & Gwynne, J. (2009). *When schools close: Effects on displaced students in Chicago Public Schools.* Chicago, IL: Consortium on Chicago School Research, University of Chicago.

Diem, S., & Welton, A.D. (2017). Disrupting spaces for education policymaking and activism. In R. Diem & Berson, M. (Eds.), *Mending walls: Historical, socio-Political, economic, and geographic perspectives.* Charlotte, NC: Information Age Publishing, Inc.

Engberg, J., Gill, B., Zamarro, G., & Zimmer, R. W. (2012). Closing schools in a shrinking district: Do student outcomes depend on which schools are closed? *Journal of Urban Economics, 71*(2), 189–203.

Ewing, E. L. (2015). "We shall not be moved": A hunger strike, education, and housing, in Chicago. *The New Yorker*. Retrieved from www.newyorker.com/news/news-desk/we-shall-not-be-moved-a-hunger-strike-education-and-housing-in-chicago

Fitzpatrick, L. (2015). Dyett hunger strike ends after 34 days. *Chicago Sun-Times*. Retrieved from https://chicago.suntimes.com/2016/6/24/18480517/dyett-hunger-strike-ends-after-34-days

Good, R. (2016). Histories that root us: Neighborhood, place, and the protest of school closures in Philadelphia. *Urban Geography, 38*(6), 861–883.

Gordon, M. F., de la Torre, M., Crowhy, J. R., Moore, P. T., Sartain, L., & Knight, D. (2018). *School closings in Chicago: Staff and student experiences and academic outcomes*. Chicago, IL: Consortium on Chicago School Research, University of Chicago. Retrieved from https://consortium.uchicago.edu/sites/default/files/2018-10/School%20Closings%20in%20Chicago-May2018-Consortium.pdf

Green, T. L. (2015). Leading for urban school reform and community development. *Educational Administration Quarterly, 51*(5), 679–711.

Hopkinson, N. (2010, September 5). Why Michelle Rhee's 'brand' failed in D.C. *The Atlantic*. Retrieved from www.theatlantic.com/politics/archive/2010/09/why-michelle-rhees-education-brand-failed-in-dc/63014/

Johnson, A. W. (2012). "Turnaround" as shock therapy: Race, neoliberalism, and school reform. *Urban Education, 48*(2), 232–256.

Journey for Justice Alliance. (2014). *Death by a thousand cuts: Racism, school closures, and public school sabotage*. Chicago, IL: Authors. Retrieved from www.issuelab.org/resources/18323/18323.pdf

Kemple, J. J. (2015). *High school closures in New York City: Impact on students' outcomes, attendance, and mobility*. New York: The Research Alliance for New York City Schools. Retrieved from https://steinhardt.nyu.edu/scmsAdmin/media/users/sg158/PDFs/hs_closures/HighSchoolClosuresinNewYorkCity_ResearchAllianceforNYCSchools_pdf.pdf

Kirshner, B., & Gaertner, M. (2015). *Review of school closures and student achievement*. Boulder, CO: National Education Policy Center. Retrieved from https://nepc.colorado.edu/thinktank/review-school-closures

Kirshner, B., Gaertner, M., & Pozzoboni, K. (2010). Tracing transitions: Understanding the impact of a school closure on displaced students. *Educational Evaluation and Policy Analysis, 32*(30), 407-429.

Kirshner, B., & Pozzoboni, K. M. (2011). Student interpretations of a school closure: Implications for student voice in equity-based school reform. *Teachers College Record, 113*(8), 1633–1667.

Lee, J., & Lubienski, C. (2017). The impact of school closures on equity of access in Chicago. *Education and Urban Society, 49*(1), 53–80.

Lipman, P. (2011). *The new political economy of urban education: Neoliberalism, race, and the right to the city*. New York: Routledge.

Lipman, P., & Hursh, D. (2007). Renaissance 2010: The reassertion of ruling-class power through neoliberal policies in Chicago. *Policy Futures in Education, 5*(2), 160–178.

Lipman, P., Vaughan, K., & Gutierrez, R. R. (2014). *Root shock: Parents' perspectives on school closings in Chicago*. Chicago, IL: Collaborative for Equity and Justice in Education, College of Education, University of Illinois at Chicago.

Masterson, M. (2016). Dyett High School reopening 1 year after activist hunger strike. *Chicago Tonight*. Retrieved from https://news.wttw.com/2016/09/01/dyett-high-school-reopening-1-year-after-activist-hunger-strike

Mead, S. (2017, April 20). The capital of education reform. *U.S. News*. Retrieved from www.usnews.com/opinion/knowledge-bank/articles/2017-04-20/michelle-rhee-set-national-example-of-education-reform-in-washington-dc

Mediratta, K., Shah, S., & McAlister, S. (2008). *Organized communities, stronger schools: A preview of research findings*. Providence, RI: Annenberg Institute for School Reform at Brown University.

The Pew Charitable Trust. (2011). *Closing public schools in Philadelphia: Lessons from six urban districts*. Retrieved from www.pewtrusts.org/-/media/assets/2011/10/19/closing_public_schools_philadelphia_report.pdf

The Pew Charitable Trust. (2016). *Governing urban schools in the future: What's facing Philadelphia and Pennsylvania*. Retrieved from www.pewtrusts.org/-/media/assets/2016/01/urban_school_governance_brief_final.pdf

Pizarek, J., Rubin, V., & Schildt, C. (2017). *An equity profile on the city of Detroit*. Washington, D.C.: Policy Link. Retrieved from www.policylink.org/resources-tools/detroit-city-equity-profile

Renée, M., & McAlister, S. (2011). Community organizing as an education reform strategy. *The Education Digest, 76*(9), 40–47.

Rothstein, R. (2017). *The color of law: A forgotten history of how our government segregated America*. New York: Liveright Publishing Corporation.

The Schott Foundation. (2013). *The color of school closures*. Quincy, MA: Authors. Retrieved from http://schottfoundation.org/blog/2013/04/05/color-school-closures

Siegel-Hawley, G., Bridges, K., & Shields, T. J. (2017). Solidifying segregation or promoting diversity? School closure and rezoning in an urban district. *Educational Administration Quarterly, 53*(1), 107–141.

Stovall, D. O. (2016). *Born out of struggle: Critical race theory, school creation, and the politics of interruption*. Albany, NY: SUNY Press.

Stovall, D. (2013). 14 souls, 19 days and 1600 dreams: Engaging critical race praxis while living on the "edge" of race. *Discourse: Studies in the Cultural Politics of Education, 34*(4), 562–579.

Strauss, V. (2017, November 29). A new D.C. schools scandal: Back to the future. *The Washington Post*. Retrieved from www.washingtonpost.com/news/answer-sheet/wp/2017/11/29/a-new-d-c-schools-scandal-back-to-the-future/?utm_term=.a4096842f379

Texas AFT. (2015). *Community schools gain traction as proven model for turning around low performing schools*. Austin, TX: Author. Retrieved from http://www.texasaft.org/community-schools-gain-traction-proven-model-turning-around-low-performing-schools/

Trujillo, T., & Valladares, M. R., & Kini, T. (2012). *Democratic school turnarounds: Pursuing equity and learning from evidence*. Boulder, CO: National Education Policy Center. Retrieved from https://nepc.colorado.edu/publication/democratic-school-turnarounds

United States Department of Education. (2003). *Questions and answers on No Child Left Behind.* Washington, D.C.: Authors. Retrieved from https://www2.ed.gov/nclb/accountability/schools/accountability.html#5

Welton, A., & Freelon, R. (2018). Community organizing as educational leadership: Lessons from Chicago on the politics of racial justice. *Journal of Research on Leadership Education, 13*(1), 79–104.

Chapter 5

Standardized Testing and the Racial Implications of Data Use

In this chapter we critically examine iterations of the Elementary Secondary Education Act (ESEA), by first reexamining the No Child Left Behind Act (NCLB) and now the most recent installment, the Every Student Succeeds Act (ESSA). We revisit lessons learned from the fall out of NCLB, and how ESSA aims to take heed of NCLB's mistakes by being more equity-centered and offering local school stakeholders more flexibility in implementation under the law. However, we find that elements of how equity is executed under ESSA still takes a color-evasive, market-oriented stance that is not much different than its predecessor, the No Child Left Behind Act (NCLB). In response, we consider how educational leaders can facilitate anti-racist approaches to ESSA, especially in regard to how they implement assessments and engage in data-use practices under the law.

In 1965, ESEA was touted as the nation's civil rights law for education as it made provisions through federal grants, like Title I, to rectify educational inequities and level the playing field for low-income students and students with disabilities (Coomer, Pearce, Dagli, Skelton, Kyser, & Thorius, 2017). ESEA's original policy intentions were equity-focused. The first iteration of the law aligned with the Johnson Administration's overall War on Poverty and broader legislative reform known as the Great Society (Zeitz, 2018). In his post-election State of the Union address, in addition to education, President Johnson called for a number of social welfare reforms such as health care for the elderly, the expansion of the Social Security program, as well as enforcement of the Civil Rights Act of 1964 followed by the Voting Rights Act of 1965

(Johnson, 1964). President Johnson, in this same noted State of the Union address, accredited poverty to "our failure to give our fellow citizens a fair chance to develop their own capacities in a lack of education and training, in a lack of medical care and housing, in a lack of decent communities in which to live and bring up their children" (Johnson, 1964, para. 25). Hence, ESEA and other Great Society reforms were seen as landmark policy moves that openly acknowledged how societal barriers make the American Dream for many an impossible goal.

ESEA also hallmarked the beginning of federal involvement in public education, which up until now had been primarily state and locally regulated and controlled (Egalite, Fusarelli, & Fusarelli, 2017). With ESEA the federal government aimed to eradicate poverty through the establishment of Title I funds and other grants directed to support increasing educational resources and opportunities for low-income students and to help build the capacity of state education agencies (Egalite et al., 2017). Originally ESEA sought to hold state and local policy actors accountable for providing equitable educational opportunities. For example, the Johnson Administration was able to use carrot and stick tactics by threatening to withdraw federal funding from southern states that refused to racially desegregate their public school systems (Frankenberg & Taylor, 2015). However, with each iteration of ESEA the federal government became progressively heavier-handed, and to date, the 13 years under No Child Left Behind (NCLB) from 2002 to 2015 marked the hardest federal grip felt by states and local school districts. Also, as we discussed in Chapter 4, we are now in an era where government officials outside of education, such as mayors and state governments, are more than just having a say in local public education matters. And in cities such as Chicago, Detroit, and New Orleans, these officials have taken over entire school districts (see Egalite et al., 2017).

Unfortunately, the national policy discourse on public education eventually veered away from the equity-based intentions of the 1965 ESEA and neoliberalism began to take a firm hold with the 1983 publication, *A Nation at Risk*, released by the Reagan Administration (U.S. NCEE, 1983). With *A Nation at Risk*, the focus was no longer on the needs of students, especially those systemically marginalized by public education, but instead on how the U.S. fared in academic performance when compared to other industrialized nations. Some of the statistics presented in *A Nation at Risk* were startling, quoting international indicators for student academic achievement that claimed the U.S. was at the bottom of the list for industrialized nations. Controversially, some of the data presented in the Reagan Administration's publication was faulty. So, the political spin fueled by *A Nation at Risk* that the American public education system was in crisis was in fact manufactured (Berliner & Biddle, 1995). In addition to this "narrative of school failure", the Reagan Administration recommended adopting academic and performance standards and state and local achievement tests that aligned with the standards (Strauss, 2018, par. 17). George H. W. Bush followed suit, positioning himself as the "Education President" during his presidential campaign and, once elected, organized a National Education Summit in 1989 of 50 state governors who were committed to developing sweeping education reforms like performance-based standards and high-stakes testing (Egalite et al., 2017). This "narrative of school failure" continued to dominate the national policy agenda on school reform up until recently, as it seems ESSA is attempting to squash the deficit discourse of public education and revert back to the original equity agenda of ESEA.

Although the first iteration of ESEA in 1965 was equity-driven, the law was relatively race-neutral in centering its agenda on students living in poverty, especially considering it was a heightened moment in the history of the Civil Rights Movement and the fight for racial equality. However, the George W. Bush Administration's 2001 reauthorization of ESEA, the No Child Left Behind Act (NCLB), endeavored to be more race-conscious by requiring states and districts to disaggregate student performance data to uncover racial inequities and get one step closer to closing the racial achievement gap. Still, NCLB used market-oriented, one-size-fits all instructional reforms such as standardized testing and punitive sanctions that were immediate fixes, not solutions that would redress systemic racial inequities in public education. As a result, NCLB reinforced racial inequities and stereotypes that blamed students from low-income families and students of color for school failure, not the system charged with serving them (Ladson-Billings, 2006; Leonardo, 2007; Milner, 2012).

NCLB AND COLOR-EVASIVE INDIVIDUALISM

While we refrain from using the word colorblind, NCLB is one example of what is known in the research on race-neutral practices as colorblind individualism. Using an anti-deficit lens, we instead coin neoliberal racism as color-evasive individualism, which is an ideology that absolves educational institutions from being held accountable for racist structures and practices (Bonilla-Silva, 2017; Leonard, 2007; Welton, Diem, & Holme, 2015). NCLB prompted states to adopt stringent test-based accountability systems that treated the achievement gap as a simple technical problem that could be resolved via instructional reforms aimed to remediate academic failure. Through this increased federal involvement schools were required to demonstrate Adequately Yearly Progress (AYP) based on the percentage of students who were proficient in the tested subject areas Math and English Language Arts, and then schools were assigned performance ratings based on the proficiency rates of various student subgroups (race/ethnicity, students eligible for free and reduced lunch, English learners, and students with disabilities) (Egalite et al., 2017).

However, NCLB generated fear of the consequences that came with a failing school performance rating. If a school was deemed low-performing for two consecutive years there were a number of possible consequences, one being reconstitution, a punitive process of replacing most of the teachers or school administrators depending on which option the district chose. At least two of the possible consequences for school failure under NCLB opened the door for private markets to sweep into public education as we discussed previously in Chapter 3 on school choice. One option was a low-performing school could be closed entirely and reopened as a charter school, or instead of closing the school its operations could instead be turned over to the state or a private company focused on school improvement and effectiveness. Even if a school did not close its doors, its low-performance rating could cause student enrollment to drop significantly by losing students who perhaps used NCLB's school choice mechanism to transfer to higher performing schools (Klein, 2015). The market-driven premise of NCLB included the fear of the consequences that come with consistent low-performance and would ultimately push schools to do whatever was necessary to boost student achievement.

As a consequence, schools in danger of failing under NCLB used prescriptive curricular and instructional practices such as teaching to the standardized test, which resulted in trying to game the system instead of fixing the broken system. Plus, because of our nation's historical and systemic disinvestment from communities of color and their schools, students at low-performing schools were primarily low-income students of color, and these students had to bear the brunt of NCLB's prescriptive, one-size-fits-all practices. Meanwhile, predominately white and affluent districts and school communities were relatively unfazed by the negative consequences of high-stakes testing.

For instance, based on the last 20 years of the National Assessment of Educational Progress (NAEP) data, gaps in achievement based on race, ethnicity, and family income remained very wide, and though they narrowed somewhat, these gaps in achievement are unlikely to close any time soon (Hansen, Levesque, Valant, & Quintero, 2018). The subtractive organizational, leadership, and instructional practices that schools with higher percentages of low-income and/or students of color endured as a result of NCLB accountability pressures only further compounded the sociopolitical stressors and injustices these schools already faced (Darling-Hammond, 2007; Fusarelli, 2004; Gay, 2007; Welton & Williams, 2015).

Still, proponents of NCLB, especially some civil rights groups, found the law to be race-conscious because it drew attention to the racial achievement gap (Egalite et al., 2017). Prior to NCLB, states and districts were not required to disaggregate their student performance data by race and other subgroups, and so the thought was that examining this data at least shed light on any gaps in student achievement, especially along racial lines. However, research on the fallout of NCLB reforms found that instead of taking the apparent racial gap in achievement as a sign of how the educational system has failed students from low-income families and students of color, the data only reinforced educators' predetermined deficit beliefs that students of color are the cause of school failure (Leonardo, 2007; Welton et al., 2015). Consequently, educators' response to NCLB mandates was to fix the student instead of trying to fix the system. Again, as an exemplar of color-evasive individualism, NCLB created a trickle-down of blame for chronic educational failure. The U.S. government was off the hook for failing to equitably support public education and in turn blamed schools and teachers, and out of fear and resentment of this blame, educators in turn blamed students from low-income families and students of color for their own oppression. NCLB used a common neoliberal strategy of placing "emphasis on efficiency and individualism" to divert "attention away from" other "social issues that need to be solved" in order to improve educational outcomes and rectify the achievement gap (Hursh, 2007, p. 305).

Since the political discourse and spectacle surrounding NCLB essentially blamed schools, teachers, and students for the failure of public education, the Bush Administration at the time was then able to divert attention away from other social problems it failed to address like inequities in access to housing, public transportation, and the lack of jobs that offer a livable wage (Hursh, 2007). Moreover, the U.S. as a neoliberal state continues to reduce funding for public education and other social services by placing greater emphasis on privatization of these services. At the same time, "to retain their legitimacy" neoliberal governments like the U.S. "do not want to appear unresponsive to social needs" (Hursh, 2007, p. 305). So, although many of the federal mandates under NCLB were unfunded, leaving states and districts to foot the bill, the political spectacle that ensued around the agenda setting for and subsequent implementation of NCLB made it seem like the Bush Administration was "doing something" about the failure of public education (Hursh, 2007, p. 306). To illustrate this point, annual federal Title I funding was supposed to increase to $25 billion by 2007, but the federal government never delivered on this promise. By 2015, the federal government only contributed $14.5 billion to Title I, over $10 billion less than its initial promise (Klein, 2015).

Consequently, NCLB failed to acknowledge the systemic origins of the racial achievement gap that are a byproduct of the long history of racial and class-based inequities in schooling. Instead, NCLB prompted mere band-aid solutions. What was and is still needed to redress the racial achievement gap is a profound restructuring and reimagining of an educational system that does right by students from low-income families and students of color. Although NCLB aimed to be a trailblazer in promoting the use of data to unmask racial inequities in the educational system, the fear that came with the punitive, market-driven reforms under the law only continued the discourse of school failure dating back to the Reagan Administration's *A Nation at Risk*. NCLB made a big splash of what ultimately became failed promises to close the achievement gap, but in the end the Bush Administration never put the money and resources towards delivering on its promises. As a market-driven mechanism, NCLB required all schools in the U.S. to bring all of their students to the proficiency level by the 2013–14 school year, and it was clear that in 2010 when only 38% of schools in the U.S. had done so, this federal directive was never going to be accomplished, especially when it goes unfunded (Klein, 2015). Right before the transition to Every Student Succeeds Act in 2015, not a single state in the U.S. got 100% of its students at proficiency or higher under NCLB (Klein, 2015).

A CALL FOR MORE FLEXIBILITY FROM NCLB

NCLB was due for reauthorization in 2007. Then, in 2008, the first Black president in U.S. history, Barack Obama, was sworn into office.

In his first term, former President Obama tried to reach across the political aisle and gain bipartisan support for policies on his agenda. However, the reauthorization of NCLB at the time competed with other politics like the Great Recession of 2008, the rise of the conservative Tea Party movement, and the long drawn out battle in Congress over the Affordable Care Act, also known as Obamacare, a policy which many conservative policy makers believed would open Pandora's box for what was then perceived as more Obama-style socialism. Furthermore, the election of the first Black president by no means meant that the U.S. was post-racial. In fact, there was an undercurrent of white resentment towards the first Black president, and this racism largely thwarted Obama's efforts to initiate deliberative, democratic bipartisanship. Thus, the confluence of political divisiveness during much of Obama's two terms as president, plus other competing priorities, further delayed the reauthorization of NCLB.

In the meantime, states and districts were still beholden to NCLB's mandates. Since the reauthorization of the law remained in queue while Congress hashed out other pressing policy issues, the Obama Administration gave states NCLB waivers to pardon them from some of the more restrictive and punitive requirements under the law (McGuinn, 2016). Forty-three states, plus the District of Columbia, received NCLB waivers (Klein, 2015). States with waivers were no longer beholden to the 2013–14 deadline for all students to achieve proficiency. Nor were schools in these states that missed their performance targets required to offer school choice or use Title I funds for tutoring (Klein, 2015). However, the perceived flexibility of NCLB waivers came with a catch. States receiving NCLB waivers either had to implement the Common Core standards or their postsecondary education institutions had to verify that the existing state standards were rigorous enough for students to be considered college and career ready (Klein, 2015; McGuinn, 2016). NCLB waiver recipients also had to develop assessments aligned with the standards, institute teacher evaluation policies tied to progress on student assessments, and require 15% of their schools in need of interventions to participate in school turnaround (Klein, 2015). The Obama Administration saw NCLB waivers as one way to have federal impact on education reform while it was still unable to get bipartisan support to reauthorize ESEA. However, conservatives viewed the granting of NCLB waivers as federal overreach and abuse of the Obama Administration's executive power (Egalite et al., 2017).

ESSA AIMS TO PROMOTE EQUITY THROUGH LESS FEDERAL OVERSIGHT

After going almost the entire two terms of his presidency without the reauthorization of ESEA, there was finally bipartisan success and President Obama signed into law the next iteration of ESEA, the Every Student Succeeds Act (ESSA), on December 10, 2015. ESSA is seen as the antithesis to the one-size-fits-all education reform, tough sanctions, and teaching to the test that transpired in the NCLB era (Wong, 2015). Thus, ESSA presumes to address the limitations of NCLB by lessening federal involvement in classrooms and returning the decision-making power to states by giving them the flexibility to design standards and assessments that meet the needs of their students (Coomer et al., 2017).

Moreover, we now have copious testimonies and research to attest to how the punitive and one-size-fits-all NCLB mandates and similar state test-based accountability systems had deficit-oriented consequences for low-income and students of color as well as their schools and teachers that were deemed failing under the law (Leonardo, 2007; McNeil, Coppola, Radigan, & Vasquez Heilig, 2008; Welton et al., 2015; Valenzuela, 2005). So, ESSA, in response, intends to be more equity-centered by allowing states and districts to develop reforms that are contextually customizable and meet the specific needs of their students.

According to Egalite et al. (2017), there are four specific ways in which ESSA centers equity while still lessening federal oversight of public education. First, ESSA disallows the Secretary of Education to use waivers as a carrot and stick that pressures states into adopting a certain set of standards like the Common Core. Second, states are no longer required to implement teacher and leader evaluations that are tied to student assessments and performance (Egalite et al., 2017). Third, states have the freedom to develop accountability systems that align with their local context and use other school performance measures that are not an indicator of student academic performance per se, but instead provide other assessments of a school's quality like student and educator engagement, school climate and safety, and student participation and completion of advanced coursework, or postsecondary readiness (Egalite, et al., 2017; Penuel, Meyer, & Valladares, 2016). Finally, the fourth way in which ESSA is seen as a more equity-centered departure from NCLB is that it is more accommodating and merciful to states' lowest-performing schools. Previously, NCLB required the 15% lowest-performing schools in states to participate in a prescriptive school turnaround process, but now under ESSA states and local districts can design interventions that are the best contextual fit for schools that represent what has now changed to the lowest 5% of schools in terms of performance (Egalite et al., 2017).

Additionally, under NCLB, schools could be financially penalized for their low performance as they were restricted in how they could use their Title I funding for interventions. Under ESSA, states can be more creative in how they use federal funding to achieve equity for students struggling academically. As such, ESSA state accountability systems must provide either of the following categories of support for chronically low-performing schools: Comprehensive Support and Improvement Schools represent the lowest 5 % of Title I schools and high schools considered dropout factories with graduation rates below 67 %; and Targeted Support and Improvement Schools are schools that have a subgroup (race, language, disability, socioeconomic status, as well as intersections of these subgroups) of students who are consistently underperforming (Ariza, King, Lewis, Smith, & Wilkins, 2017). Districts are required to develop improvement plans for either category of schools and then states must set performance thresholds for schools to achieve and eventually exit one of these categories (Ariza et al., 2017). One final category, the Additional Targeted Support and Improvement Schools, comprises schools that have one or more subgroups with performance so low that if all the students in the subgroup were in itself a school then they could be classified as a Comprehensive Improvement School. Schools in this latter category must develop district approved plans to redress resource inequities (Ariza et al., 2017).

DOES ESSA FOLLOW THROUGH ON ITS CLAIMS FOR EQUITY?

While ESSA loosens the federal grip, the jury is still out as to whether the implementation of the law will be more equitable than NCLB (Wong, 2015). Like NCLB, ESSA still requires that students in grades 3 and 8 are tested, and then tested once again in high school (Egalite et al., 2017). ESSA also requires elementary and middle grades to be proficient on the state test, have English language proficiency, demonstrate student growth, and satisfy at least one of the school quality indicators (Egalite et al., 2017; Penuel et al., 2016). While including non-academic indicators for accountability measures is a step in the right direction, ESSA still requires state accountability systems to give more weight to academic indicators than non-academic indicators of school quality (Penuel et al., 2016).

With the initial rollout of ESSA, states were required to develop state plans for how they would execute the law, but early on most states' plans were considered to be weak in terms of their outlook on equity. Some states proposed strategies in their plans that were no different than what they had previously promised in their application for an NCLB waiver (Forte, 2018). Under Secretary of Education Devos's leadership, the U.S. Department of Education is approving states' plans without holding them accountable for ESSA's requirements that equity be the emphasis and mainstay of their plans. The dilemma is how to strike the balance between giving states and districts more flexibility, less federal oversight, and thus more freedom to emphasize equity while at the same time holding them accountable for centering equity. For example, even with power again entrusted to states and school districts, American Indian and Alaskan Native educational leaders have concerns that State Education Agencies (SEA) and Local Education Agencies (LEA) will not partner and contract with tribes if ESSA does not require them to do so (Mackey, 2017). So, unfortunately with ESSA, SEAs and LEAs have control over whether to partner with and the nature of their partnership with tribes (Mackey, 2017).

There are ongoing critiques of how states have used the flexibility of ESSA to instead renege on equity (Forte, 2018). Recently, the National Urban League (2019) rated the state ESSA plans for equity indicators and found that slightly over half (54%) of the 36 states and the District of Columbia evaluated were *sufficient*, whereas 9 were *excellent* and 8 were rated as *poor*. The National Urban League's evaluation focused on 12 equity indicators, some of which included: goals and indicators, educator equity, stakeholder engagement, breaking the school-to-prison pipeline, equitable access to early childhood learning, equitable implementation of college and career standards, out-of-school time learning, equitable access to high quality curricula, and clear reporting and transparent data systems. While each state's ranking was based on the weighted average performance for each of the indicators, the following three indicators were weighted more heavily as they were seen as especially critical to promoting and achieving equity: (1) subgroup performance, (2) supports and interventions for struggling schools, and (3) resource equity. What seemed to be the area most in need of improvement was that of providing supports and interventions for struggling schools; 14 states received a poor rating for this equity indicator (National Urban League, 2019; Schaffhauser, 2019). The report uncovered how some states in their ESSA plans were purposefully reducing the number of schools identified as needing improvement so then additional resources would not need to be directed to these schools. In addition, some placed less emphasis on critically examining subgroup performance, and others left it up to districts entirely to decide how to identify and respond to inequities. But if states water down the equity focus of their ESSA plans in these ways, then the result is that the only resources they provide to districts to redress inequities are monitoring and ensuring districts comply to the law (National Urban League, 2019; Schaffhauser, 2019). Consequently, it seems that most states' commitment to equity under ESSA is still rather weak.

RECOMMENDATIONS: ANTI-RACIST DISCUSSIONS ABOUT ASSESSMENTS AND DATA

At this stage of implementation, ESSA does need to be formatively evaluated and then recalibrated to ensure that local policy actors are accountable for promoting equity under the spirit of the law. Still, it is a cause for optimism that states and school districts have the freedom to design assessments and use the data gleaned as a result to be more intentional in their approaches to redressing inequity. However, as was learned from NCLB, if educators' racial biases go unchecked when discussing assessments, the decisions based on this data can do more harm to students from low-income families and students of color than good. For example, a study on teachers' perceptions of student achievement data found that teachers attributed student performance to their instruction only 15% of the time, and were more likely to attribute performance to student characteristics like race, gender, or their socioeconomic status (Evans, Teasdale, Gannon-Slater, La Londe, Crenshaw, Greene, & Schwandt, 2019). More specifically, 32% of teachers' explanations of student performance were based on behavioral characteristics of the student, such as student attitudes or lack of attention. Essentially, educators primarily positioned students as the cause of their own academic struggles and did not consider how the educational policies and structures may in fact be a disservice to students.

Hence, we recommend that district and school level leaders undertake ongoing professional development and coaching that encourages educators to critically unpack the racial biases they carry when engaging in discussions about student performance on any type of assessment. We as educators hold our students' educational pathways and destinies in the palm of our hands when we use data from assessments to make decisions that drive the design of educational policies, structures, and practices. Yet, when educators use an anti-racist lens to drive discussions around data, data-driven decision-making (DDDM) can then be a starting point to uncovering systemic level inequities that were not always clearly visible (Myers & Finnigan, 2018). One framework we find particularly useful in encouraging educators to have difficult discussions about their racial biases when engaging in DDDM is Myers and Finnigan's (2018) ERASE framework (an acronym) that includes the following five steps: (1) **E**xamine and start to disaggregate various types of data; (2) **R**aise questions that help educators identify what differential outcomes they notice and how these outcomes are tied to racial biases and structural racism; (3) **A**scertain root causes that explain the differential outcomes and brainstorm research-based solutions to address; (4) **S**elect and prioritize short-term and long-term strategies and solutions; and (5) **E**valuate progress by reexamining data sets and making any necessary adjustments to policies and practice in response.

Also, school leaders should question what types of data they are using to drive anti-racist changes in their school communities. There is an emerging body of research in educational leadership that considers students, parents, and community members from minoritized groups as equal partners in school leadership. We should also see these stakeholders as collaborators in developing assessments and bring them to the table when we are having discussions about data, as they have important cultural knowledge about the school community that would be integral to facilitating anti-racist change system-wide (Ishimaru, 2013; Rodela & Bertrand, 2018; Kennedy & Datnow, 2011). Therefore, we suggest that effective facilitators of anti-racist dialogue also need to be willing to steer the conversation away from blaming the students by asking practitioners tough questions about how they use data to assess student learning and achievement such as, "What ways are our practices failing such-and-such students?" and then begin to "unlearn to ask what is wrong with these students" (Bensimon, 2012, p. 34) in order to get to the root of the problem.

DISCUSSION QUESTIONS

1. Take a look at your state's ESSA plan. How is your state's ESSA plan a strong advocate for equity and in what ways may the plan be missing the mark in terms of equity and why?

2. If you were a parent or educator during the implementation of NCLB, in your opinion how was racial equity framed under the law? Do you think NCLB worked to promote racial equity?
3. Is your district and/or school engaging in discussions about racial equity, and how, if at all, is ESSA framing these discussions?
4. ESSA intends to provide states and districts with more freedom and flexibility from federal oversight. Do you think this is actually happening on the ground in your daily work as an educational leader? Have you faced any obstacles in your daily work as a result of ESSA?
5. Does ESSA's flexibility and freedom from federal oversight promote equity, especially in terms of developing assessments to meet the context-specific needs of your district and school community?
6. What types of assessments are you developing and implementing, and who (e.g., administrators, teachers, parents, students, community members) is involved in the design and discussion around these assessments, and why? Are there certain perspectives missing from assessment design and data discussions? What can you do to ensure those holding these perspectives are equal partners in data-driven decision-making?
7. How are you dialoguing about data with your district and/or school community? Are there any biases in hindsight that you may carry when engaging in these discussions about data? Also, how are you using data to think about how racial inequities emerge systemically? Are you using an anti-deficit approach that does not blame racially minoritized students for the inequities in educational opportunities they experience daily?
8. What types of professional development and ongoing coaching are your receiving for anti-racist approaches to data-driven decision-making?

ESSA RESOURCES

- Council of Chief State School Officers: https://ccsso.org/taxonomy/term/151
- Education Commission of the States: www.ecs.org/every-student-succeeds-act-essa-resources/
- The Education Trust: https://edtrust.org/resource/the-every-student-succeeds-act-whats-in-it-what-does-it-mean-for-equity/

- National Association of Elementary School Principals: www.naesp.org/essa
- National Association of Secondary School Principals: www.nassp.org/policy-advocacy-center/resources/essa-toolkit/essa-fact-sheets/every-student-succeeds-act-essa-overview/
- National Conference of State Legislators: www.ncsl.org/ncsl-in-dc/standing-committees/education/every-student-succeeds-act-essa-information-and-resources.aspx
- National PTA: www.pta.org/home/advocacy/federal-legislation/Every-Student-Succeeds-Act-ESSA

RECOMMENDED READINGS

Darling-Hammond, L., Bae, S., Cook-Harvey, C. M., Lam, L., Mercer, C., Podolsky, A., Stosich, A. (2016). *Pathways to new accountability through the Every Student Succeeds Act.* Palo Alto, CA: Learning Policy Institute.

Datnow, A., & Park, V. (2014). *Data-driven leadership.* San Francisco, CA: Jossey-Bass.

Fernández, E., LeChasseur, K., & Weiner, J. (2017). Introduction. *Educational Administration Quarterly, 53*(5), 699–704. Special Issue: Implications and Consequences of ESSA: Exploring the Changing Landscape of Federal Policy and Educational Administration.

National Urban League. (2019). *Standards of equity and excellence: A lens of ESSA state plans.* New York: Author. Retrieved from http://ncos.iamempowered.com/pdf/ESSA%20Full%20Report.pdf

REFERENCES

Ariza, G., King, L., Lewis, T., Smith, A., & Wilkins, J. (2017). *Every Student Succeeds Act (ESSA) guide for advocates: How you can ensure ESSA implementation helps to build more equitable schools.* Washington, D.C.: The Leadership Conference Education Fund. Retrieved from http://civilrightsdocs.info/pdf/education/ESSA/ESSA-Guide.pdf

Bensimon, E. M. (2012). The equity scorecard: Theory of change. In E. M. Bensimon & L. E. Malcolm (Eds.), *Confronting equity issues on campus: Implementing the equity scorecard in theory and practice* (pp. 17–44). Sterling, VA: Stylus Publishing, LLC.

Berliner, D. C., & Biddle, B. J. (1995). *The manufactured crisis: Myths, fraud, and the attack on America's public schools.* Reading, MA: Addison-Wesley.

Bonilla-Silva, E. (2017). *Racism without racists: Color-blind racism and the persistence of racial inequality in America* (5th edition). Lanham, MD: Rowman & Littlefield.

Coomer, M. N, Pearce, N., Dagli, C., Skelton, S. M., Kyser, T. S., & Thorius, K. A. K. (2017). The legacy of Civil Rights in the Every Student Succeeds Act. *Equity Dispatch*. Indianapolis, IN: Midwest & Plains Equity Assistance Center (MAP EAC). Retrieved from: http://glec.education.iupui.edu/Images/Newsletters/Equity/Dispatch.pdf

Darling-Hammond, L. (2007). Race, inequality and educational accountability: The irony of 'No Child Left Behind'. *Race Ethnicity and Education, 10*(3), 245–260.

Egalite, A. J., Fusarelli, L. D., & Fusarelli, B. C. (2017). Will decentralization affect educational inequity? The Every Student Succeeds Act. *Educational Administration Quarterly, 53*(5), 757–781.

Evans, M., Teasdale, R. M., Gannon-Slater, N., La Londe, P. G., Crenshaw, H. L., Greene, J. C., & Schwandt, T. A. (2019). How did that happen? Teachers' explanations for low test scores. *Teachers College Record, 121*(2), 1–40.

Forte, D. (2018). *Under ESSA, achieving equity in education is still challenging*. New York: The Century Foundation. Retrieved from https://tcf.org/content/commentary/essa-achieving-equity-education-still-challenging/?session=1

Frankenberg, E., & Taylor, K. (2015). ESEA and the Civil Rights Act: An interbranch approach to furthering desegregation. *The Russel Sage Foundation Journal of the Social Sciences, 1*(3), 32–49.

Fusarelli, L. D. (2004). The potential impact of the No Child Left Behind Act on equity and diversity in American education. *Educational Policy, 18*(1), 71–94.

Gay, G. (2007). The rhetoric and reality of NCLB. *Race Ethnicity and Education, 10*(3), 279–293.

Hansen, M., Levesque, E. M., Valant, J., & Quintero, D. (2018). *2018 Brown Center Report on American education: Trends in NAEP math, reading, and civics scores*. Washington, D.C.: The Brookings Institution. Retrieved from www.brookings.edu/research/2018-brown-center-report-on-american-education-trends-in-naep-math-reading-and-civics-scores/

Hursh, D. (2007) Exacerbating inequality: The failed promise of the No Child Left Behind Act. *Race Ethnicity and Education, 10*(3), 295–308.

Ishimaru, A. (2013). From heroes to organizers: Principals and education organizing in urban school reform. *Educational Administration Quarterly, 49*(1), 3–51.

Johnson, L. B. (1964). *January 8, 1964: State of the Union*. Charlottesville, VA: University of Virginia Miller Center. Retrieved from https://millercenter.org/the-presidency/presidential-speeches/january-8-1964-state-union

Kennedy, B. L,. & Datnow, A. (2011). Student involvement and data-driven decision making: Developing a new typology. *Youth and Society, 43*(4), 1246–1271.

Klein, A. (2015, April 10). No Child Left Behind: An overview. *Education Week*. Retrieved from www.edweek.org/ew/section/multimedia/no-child-left-behind-overview-definition-summary.html#Proficiency

Ladson-Billings, G. (2006). From the achievement gap to the education debt: Understanding achievement in U.S. schools. *Educational Researcher, 35*(7), 3–12.

Leonardo, Z. (2007). The war on schools: NCLB, nation creation and the educational construction of whiteness. *Race Ethnicity and Education, 10*(3), 261–278.

Mackey, H. J. (2017). The ESSA in Indian Country: Problematizing self-determination through the relationships between federal, state, and tribal governments. *Educational Administration Quarterly, 53*(5), 782–808.

McNeil, L. M., Coppola, E., Radigan, J., & Vasquez Heilig, J. (2008). Avoidable losses: High stakes accountability and the dropout crisis. *Education Policy Analysis Archives, 16*(3). Retrieved from http://epaa.asu.edu/epaa/v16n3/

McGuinn, P. (2016). From No Child Left Behind to the Every Student Succeeds Act: Federalism and the education legacy of the Obama Administration. *Publius: The Journal of Federalism, 46*(3), 392–415.

Milner IV, H. R. (2012). Beyond a test score: Explaining opportunity gaps in educational practice. *Journal of Black Studies, 43*(6), 693–718.

Myers, L. C., & Finnigan, K. S. (2018). Using data to guide difficult conversations around structural racism. *Voices in Urban Education, 48*, 38–45. Retrieved from http://vue.annenberginstitute.org/sites/default/files/pageContent/VUE48_Myers.pdf

National Urban League. (2019). *Standards of equity and excellence: A lens of ESSA state plans.* New York: Author. Retrieved from http://ncos.iamempowered.com/pdf/ESSA%20Full%20Report.pdf

Penuel, W., Meyer, E., & Valladares, M. R. (2016). *Making the most of the Every Student Succeeds Act (ESSA). Helping schools focus on school equity, quality, and climate.* Boulder, CO: National Education Policy Center. Retrieved from https://nepc.colorado.edu/publication/ESSA

Rodela, K. C., & Bertrand, M. (2018). Rethinking educational leadership in the margins: Youth, parent and community leadership for equity and social justice. *Journal of Research on Leadership Education, 13*(1), 3–9.

Schaffhauser, D. (2019, May 5). Just half of State ESSA Plans are sufficient in terms of equity standards. *The Journal.* Retrieved from https://thejournal.com/articles/2019/05/06/just-half-of-state-essa-plans-are-sufficient-in-terms-of-equity-standards.aspx

Strauss, V. (2018, April 26). 'A Nation at Risk' demanded education reform 35 years ago. Here's how it's been bungled ever since. *The Washington Post.* Retrieved from www.washingtonpost.com/news/answer-sheet/wp/2018/04/26/the-landmark-a-nation-at-risk-called-for-education-reform-35-years-ago-heres-how-it-was-bungled/?utm_term=.4b8991d8bbac

United States National Commission on Excellence in Education. (1983). *A nation at risk: the imperative for educational reform.* Washington, D.C.: The National Commission on Excellence in Education.

Valenzuela, A. (2005). *Leaving children behind: How "Texas-style" accountability fails Latino youth.* Albany, NY: SUNY Press.

Welton, A., & Williams, M. (2015). Accountability strain, college-readiness drain: Sociopolitical tensions involved in maintaining a college-going culture in a high "minority," high poverty Texas high school. *The High School Journal, 98*(2), 181–204.

Welton, A. D., Diem, S., & Holme, J. J. (2015). Color conscious, cultural blindness: Suburban school districts and demographic change. *Education and Urban Society, 47*(6), 695–722.

Wong, A. (2015, December 9). The bloated rhetoric of No Child Left Behind's demise. *The Atlantic.* Retrieved from www.theatlantic.com/education/archive/2015/12/the-bloated-rhetoric-of-no-child-left-behinds-demise/419688/

Zeitz, J. (2018, January 28). What everyone gets wrong about LBJ's Great Society. *Politico Magazine.* Retrieved from www.politico.com/magazine/story/2018/01/28/lbj-great-society-josh-zeitz-book-216538

Chapter 6

School Funding and the Need for Resource Redistribution

Money matters in public education. It helps to improve educational opportunities and can lead to resource allocation that is more equal. Indeed, when states commit to financially investing in public education, students are more likely to better perform academically while in school *and* they are more likely later on in life to earn higher wages in the workforce (Baker et al., 2018). Yet, the way current education systems are set up in many states allows funding disparities to persist across school communities (Leachman, 2019). Public school districts, particularly those that have a student population that is primarily low-income, are consistently underfunded, and many school districts across the U.S., almost a third, are spending more money on districts serving wealthier students (Farrie, Kim, & Sciarra, 2019). Indeed, as Darling-Hammond (2019) states, "Public schools in the United States are among the most inequitably funded of any in the industrialized world" (p. 1). Moreover, as public school enrollment continues to rise, demographics shift, and income inequality and segregation persists (see Chapter 2), states are finding it harder to fund schools and their students' needs and the funding decisions being made primarily at the local level can exacerbate these existent school inequities (Leachman, 2019). And while race may not be explicitly discussed in issues such as local control, resource redistribution, and how to effectively expend resources, it undergirds all of these issues (Ryan, 1999). Further, when states decide to change their school funding formulas and less money is allocated to districts, it becomes increasingly challenging for schools to address needs like overcrowded classrooms, teacher quality, or improving student outcomes (Leachman & Figueroa, 2019).

School leaders are in the difficult position of trying to navigate the budgetary constraints placed on them by state policy makers' decisions on how to fund public schools. A recent survey conducted by *Education Week* shows that school administrators feel that their "budgets are being squeezed between political pressures with amounts dictated by outdated spending mandates and a cash flow that is insufficient and unpredictable," which in turn, makes it very difficult for them to engage in any forward budget planning and has even led to some districts going through their savings (Burnette, 2019b, p. 3). Additionally, a recent report showed that some states are not even providing the state aid that is required of them under their own funding formulas (Farrie et al., 2019). In response, teachers have protested and gone on strike across the nation and lawsuits have mounted to challenge systems that are inadequately and unfairly funding public schools.

In the 2015–16 school year, the U.S. spent approximately $12,000 per student on public education, $706 billion total, of which only 8% came from federal sources, which is primarily for students with special needs and low-income students (Farrie et al., 2019; McFarland et al., 2019). While approximately the same percentage of education revenue comes from state (47%) and local sources (45%), we are seeing a growth in the contribution of local sources to total revenues, increasing by almost 30% from 2000–16 (McFarland et al., 2019). As we look at the status of education funding nationwide, according to recent research by the Center on Budget and Policy Priorities, state and local funding in 22 states plus the District of Columbia remains below pre-2008 Great Recession levels. In the 2017 school year, state and local funding was at least 10% below pre-Great Recession levels in seven states. In Florida and Arizona, where the deepest education cuts have occurred, funding was down by over 22 % (Leachman, 2019). As states continue to cut funding for public education, operational costs (e.g., transportation and facilities, staffing, salaries/benefits, and student costs) continue to rise as the need for special services to support a growing diverse student population (see Chapter 2, e.g., more English learners, students with disabilities, low-income students) also increases (Burnette, 2019a). Further, as schools rely heavily on local revenues to operate, unsurprisingly schools remain woefully unequal by income and race. Moreover, school and district leaders worry that if another recession occurs, the effects may be even worse for their districts than they were following the 2008 Great Recession (Burnette, 2019b).

In the U.S., local property tax is the key driver of school funding. At the local level, 81% of education revenues come from local property taxes (McFarland et al., 2019). As property tax bases are higher in neighborhoods with higher housing values, and because high levels of residential segregation by socioeconomic status exist, relying on local property taxes to fund schools creates an unequal distribution of wealth among school districts (Jackson, Johnson, & Persico, 2016)--property-wealthy districts have access to more resources while low-income districts are all but left behind. Furthermore, there is a lack of recognition of how federal housing policy, blockbusting, and redlining are responsible for ongoing housing discrimination, which is directly connected to property wealth, race, and subsequently school wealth and racial make-up (Rothstein, 2017). According to a 2019 EdBuild report, "on the whole, a student living within the geographic boundaries of a primarily White school district in the United States has a resource advantage over those enrolled in a heavily nonwhite system, regardless of geographic location or wealth" (p. 4). The report goes on to say,

> Nationally, predominately White school districts get $23 billion more than their nonwhite peers, despite serving a similar number of children. White school districts average revenue receipts of almost $14,000 per student, but nonwhite districts receive only $11,682. That's a divide of over $2,200 on average, per student.
> (EdBuild, 2019, p. 4)

It is worth repeating that a *$23 billion funding gap* exists between white and nonwhite school districts in the United States. Yet, if we look back to how the education system was set up based on the idea of local control and leaving it up to local communities to make decisions about their schools (EdBuild, 2019), our current inequitable funding situation is not all that surprising. Further, although there has been some success in the courts when it comes to school finance equity, in many cases "the courts did not make a distinction between local taxes and local governance of schools," which "further entrenched the idea that spending on school districts is an entitlement of local governance" (EdBuild, 2019, p. 1). This is further compounded by school leaders' beliefs that the biggest challenge to funding in their districts and to making decisions that are in the best interest of their students is elected officials (Education Week Research Center, 2019). And so, here we are today still operating within a system that favors local control, which coupled with lawmakers' inability to adequately fund schools and persistent residential segregation, results in schools where the student population is primarily nonwhite continuing to receive the least funding.

In this chapter, we provide an overview of how school funding has been litigated over time in the U.S. and how this has impacted current school funding policies, the relationship between school funding and race, and examples of school finance reform policies and programs in states and local school districts being implemented to provide more opportunities to students in low-income, racially segregated schools. In order to understand the different levels of funding and resources that exist between school districts—white and nonwhite—school leaders must be cognizant of why these disparities occurred in the first place, how they are racialized, and what they can do moving forward to create equitable school environments.

SCHOOL FINANCE LITIGATION

School finance litigation has been pursued as a way for marginalized students to attain equal educational opportunity (Green, Baker, & Oluwole, 2008). It is one avenue, in addition to legislative actions such as ESEA, NCLB, and ESSA (see Chapter 5), that has been used for decades to remedy unequal school funding and establish parity among school districts. Additionally, many of the school finance cases have brought to light deep-seated racial issues that allow educational opportunity gaps to endure (Hinojosa, 2016). Yet, because the U.S. Supreme Court determined that education is not a fundamental right explicitly stated in the U.S. Constitution, and therefore wealth-based discrimination is not occurring via funding in school districts (see *San Antonio Independent School District v. Rodriguez,* 1973), in many states the battle over the imbalance in school funding is still ongoing. States play a central role in school funding; their constitutions explicitly communicate what rights to an education should look like. In the last 40 years, lawsuits on inequitable school funding and educational opportunity have been filed in 45 of 50 states, with plaintiffs succeeding in about 60% of these cases (Rebell, 2017). In 34 of the lawsuits, the question as to whether more funding leads to better education has been clearly established, putting to rest the false myth that more money does not help educational outcomes (Rebell, 2017). Indeed, in many state courts, legislative action has been required to redress inequitable educational opportunities and disparities between low-wealth and affluent districts (Jackson et al., 2016), albeit with mixed outcomes.

In this section we highlight just a few of the many school finance cases that have been argued across the United States. We specifically chose these cases—*Serrano v. Priest* (1971), *San Antonio Independent School District v. Rodriguez* (1973), *Edgewood Independent School District v. Kirby* (1989), *Abbott v. Burke* (1985–2011), *Rose v. Council for Better Education* (1989), *Campaign for Fiscal Equity v. State of New York* (2001–2006), *Martinez v. New Mexico* (2018)—as many are considered landmark school finance cases related to educational opportunity, occurred in various geographical contexts, and show how over time, the differences in arguments being made—equity vs. adequacy—against inequitable education funding systems. That is, which we discuss below, from the 1970 to the mid-1980s, equity was used to argue that states were responsible for remedying local financing issues to provide all children with a quality education. From the late 1980s onward, since most state constitutions have provisions outlining adequate levels of education that must be provided to children, it was argued that low spending levels in districts meant that the state was not meeting this adequate requirement (Jackson et al., 2016). Some argue that some more recent cases have sought to tackle inequities connected to issues such as race (Hinojosa, 2016). Below we discuss these cases in detail so that school leaders can better understand the historical context in which school funding battles are situated and how, in the current color-evasive, market-driven education context, we may think about school funding systems and what is needed to truly create school systems that are equitably resourced and of high quality.

Serrano v. Priest

The *Serrano v. Priest* (1971) case was one of the first and widely known school funding equity cases brought to state court. In the case, students and families in Los Angeles County public schools argued that the state's property tax-based school finance system disadvantaged students in low-income districts and the educational opportunities afforded to them. The California Supreme Court agreed and ruled that the state's school finance system violated the Equal Protection clause and was therefore unconstitutional. The court went on to order the state to equalize property tax rates and revenues to assist in closing the funding disparities across districts. The ruling was important as it shifted the way schools were funded in California from local to state control. Yet, despite the court's ruling and the state coming close to achieving equitable per-pupil funding for almost all of its students, two things occurred that turned this progress around. First, in 1978, California residents passed Proposition 13, which froze property tax levels at their 1976 assessed levels, and capped ad valorem tax rates at 1% of cash value at the time of their purchase. Proposition 13 was devastating for California school districts as property taxes now limited the ability to equalize school funding; it would be up to the state to assist districts in achieving equal funding. However, the state did not decide to increase education expenditures and instead actually lowered them, which was the second dagger to the *Serrano* ruling.

In recent years, California has tried to address school funding by creating a new funding formula that is not based on property taxes and provides additional resources for schools with more students who are low-income, English learners, and/or have a disability (Martin, Boser, & Benner, 2018). The Local Control Funding Formula (LCFF) was authorized in 2013 and, according to the California Department of Education (2019), the new funding formula, which overhauled a system that had been in place for about 40 years, is different as it "establishes base, supplemental, and concentration grants in place of the myriad of previously existing K-12 funding streams, including revenue limits, general purpose block grants, and most of the 50-plus state categorical programs that existed at the time" (n.p.). A recent study by the Learning Policy Institute found that California's new school finance system is having positive results for academic outcomes and graduation rates across all school districts. And specifically, the additional funding that has been afforded to high poverty districts through the LCFF has led to significant academic improvements for students from low-income families and students of color (Johnson & Tanner, 2018).

San Antonio Independent School District v. Rodriguez

In 1968, a group of parents led by Demetrio Rodriguez, a longtime equal rights community activist, filed a lawsuit against the Edgewood Independent School District, a low-income, predominately Latinx district in San Antonio, Texas, and six other school districts, arguing that the state's school finance system was inequitable. Specifically, the argument at the center of the case was the notion that education is a federal right as it is necessary in order to be an engaged citizen. Moreover, as the Texas state school finance system relied on local property tax for school funding, districts like Edgewood that are located in predominately low-income areas have low tax bases and are therefore underfunded and underresourced, which impacts necessary levels of education provided to students. As a result, children in low-wealth school districts are at an extreme disadvantage as compared to their peers in wealthier school districts. The case eventually made its way all the way to the U.S. Supreme Court where, in a five–four ruling, the justices decided that the system did not violate the Equal Protection Clause as Texas was not refusing to provide education to low-income students *and* the U.S. Constitution does not specifically state education to be a fundamental right (*San Antonio Independent School District v. Rodriguez*, 1973). The Court also stated "whether there is a correlation between expenditures and education quality is not one the federal courts should consider" (Rebell, 2017, p. 186). Since the *Rodriguez* ruling, there have been seven court cases with Texas school districts suing over the state's finance system that have reached the Texas Supreme Court and the Edgewood district is still inequitably funded (Swaby & Ura, 2018). In the state's most recent case, two-thirds of Texas school districts claimed that the current finance system does not meet the adequacy and suitability requirements outlined in the Texas Constitution. In its ruling, the Texas Supreme Court upheld the school funding system with one of the Justice's stating in the opinion, "Our Byzantine school funding 'system' is undeniably imperfect, with immense room for improvement. But it satisfies minimum constitutional requirements" (*Morath v. Texas Taxpayer & Student Fairness Coalition*, 2016, p. 99). Multiple states have also tried to overturn *Rodriguez* but have been unsuccessful or the cases remain outstanding (Martin et al., 2018).

Edgewood Independent School District v. Kirby

Following the *Rodriguez* ruling, in 1984 the Mexican American Legal Defense and Educational Fund filed a suit on behalf of the Edgewood Independent School arguing that the Texas school finance system and its reliance on local property taxes to fund schools was discriminatory and inequitable. When the case began, there were 21 parents and eight school districts involved; this number grew to 67 additional school districts and several other parents and students (The Texas Politics Project, n.d.). In 1989, the Texas Supreme Court ruled the finance system as unconstitutional, noting that property wealth per student in Edgewood ISD was considerably lower than Alamo Heights Independent School District, one of the wealthiest districts in the same county as Edgewood and the state of Texas. The court ordered the state legislature to devise an equitable system by the 1990–91 school year.

The Texas Legislature created a plan that became known as the "Robin Hood" plan, in which money would be redistributed from affluent districts to low-wealth districts in order to equalize funding. While Texas was able to reduce funding disparities between affluent and low-wealth districts, the Robin Hood plan proved unpopular and problematic among Texans. Property-wealthy districts who were set to lose money over the plan argued it was illegal and eventually the court sided with them. In 1993, a new plan was signed into law in which school districts would seek to equalize funding through one of five options:

> (1) merging its tax base with a poorer district, (2) sending money to the state to help pay for students in poorer districts, (3) contracting to educate students in other districts, (4) consolidating voluntarily with one or more districts, or (5) transferring some of its commercial taxable property to another district's tax rolls.
>
> (The Texas Politics Project, n.d.)

Over time, as previously stated, there would be many iterations of the *Edgewood* case argued over equitable, and later on, adequate school funding in Texas. Yet, as state funding for education declined and, as previously mentioned, the Texas Supreme Court eventually ruled that while the system may be "undeniably imperfect" it meets the basic requirements as set forth in the state constitution, disparities continue for students in Edgewood (Swaby & Ura, 2018).

Abbott v. Burke

The *Abbott v. Burke* case began a new wave of approaching school funding issues through an adequacy framework, which in some cases let states off the hook for providing students the bare minimum when it came to per-pupil funding. However, in *Abbott*, what made the decision considered to be a success was the ability to define the level of funding and resources needed to provide equitable educational opportunity (Martin et al., 2018). In 1981, the New Jersey Education Law Center filed a complaint on behalf of 20 children attending New Jersey public schools across four cities—Camden, East Orange, Irvington, and Jersey City—arguing that the state's finance system disadvantaged students in these low-income districts and that funding disparities contributed to the districts' inability to provide an adequate education. The New Jersey Supreme Court ruled the finance system to be unconstitutional and directed the state legislature to implement a funding system that would ensure urban districts (31 in total) received funding equivalent to that of wealthier districts. While the initial *Abbott* ruling and subsequent mandates put New Jersey in the spotlight as the only state to equalize education resources between low-wealth and affluent districts, there would later be numerous motions filed in the court around the timing of the ruling's implementation and other disagreements (Education Law Center, 2019). However, the court's consistency in enforcing funding equalization as well as providing more resources to underresourced schools, and even recently focusing on school quality, has assisted in improving conditions in low-income districts (Martin et al., 2018).

Rose v. Council for Better Education

While the *Abbott* case saw the beginning of approaching school funding litigation through an adequacy lens, *Rose v. Council for Better Education* became the leading and most recognized adequacy case in the United States. Indeed, since the *Rose* decision, adequacy has been a key feature in school funding cases. In 1989, the Kentucky Supreme Court found that the state's finance system was in violation of its constitution and that every student should be provided with an adequate education. The court also acknowledged that education is a fundamental right under the state's constitution. The decision led to the state completely overhauling its education system. In this new system, the court ruled that the goal should be for students to become "sufficient" in the following:

(1) oral and written communication skills to function in a complex and changing society;
(2) knowledge of economic, social, and political systems so that informed choices can be made;
(3) understanding of governmental processes to become engaged citizens;
(4) understanding of mental and physical well-being for oneself and others;
(5) grounding in the arts to be appreciative of cultural and historical heritage;
(6) training or preparation for advanced training in academic or vocational fields; and

(7) academic or vocational skills to be able to compete in academics or the job market. (Education Law Center, 2019, n.p.)

The Kentucky Legislature responded with the 1990 Kentucky Education Reform Act (KERA), a sweeping reform that brought changes to finance, governance, and curriculum. Since KERA was implemented, an additional 26 states have enacted school funding reforms (Lafortune, Rothstein, & Schanzenbach, 2016).

Campaign for Fiscal Equity v. State of New York

In another case based on adequate funding, in 1993, the Campaign for Fiscal Equity, a non-profit organization created by parents to protect and promote New York students' basic educational rights, filed a lawsuit claiming the New York school finance system was unconstitutional due to its underfunding of New York City schools. As a result of the underfunding, students were being denied their right to an "opportunity" for a "sound basic education," defined as "a meaningful high school education, one which prepares [young people] to function productively as civic participants" under the state constitution (*Campaign for Fiscal Equity v. State of New York*, 2003, p. 26). After 13 years, the Court of Appeals eventually ordered New York to ensure that a funding system was in place to provide students with an adequate education. Yet, the timing of the decision could not have been worse as the U.S. was experiencing an economic crisis due to the Great Recession of 2008. Similar to other states, budget cuts were made in New York that caused school funding to decrease and none of the funds owed under the lawsuit were ever provided. Advocates argue that schools in New York are still owed over $4 billion (Disare, 2018).

Yazzie/Martinez v. State of New Mexico

One final, and very recent, school finance case we highlight is the *Yazzie/Martinez v. State of New Mexico* (2018). According to Hinojosa (2016), the *Yazzie/Martinez* case is different from its predecessors as it takes a more comprehensive approach to challenging inequitable educational opportunity and looking at inequities as they connect to race, ethnicity, and language in addition to arguing for students with more needs. In 2014, families and school districts in New Mexico sued the state's department of education for not providing a sufficient education system to all children in the state—particularly Native American, English learner (EL), low-income, and students with disabilities—as required by the New Mexico State Constitution and the resources needed to succeed academically (Hinojosa, 2016). Four years later, in July 2018, a New Mexico judge ruled that the state was failing to comply with the state constitution (New Mexico Center on Law and Poverty, 2018). Specifically, the state was found to not be in compliance with state and federal laws around the education of EL and Native American students, including the New Mexico Indian Education Act, Bilingual Multicultural Education Act, and the Hispanic Education Act. The state was also found to not be in compliance with providing students with programs and services to prepare them to be college and career ready, and was not providing the correct oversight of the programs and services. The judge ordered the state to come up with the funding needed to provide New Mexico students with a sufficient education that would help prepare them for college and the workforce (NM Center on Law and Poverty, 2018). The case addresses the numerous systemic issues that prevent students from receiving a sufficient education, including lack of necessary resources and monitoring how funding that was received was spent, as well as curricular issues such as bilingualism and multiculturalism. While past school finance cases have focused more on equity and adequacy of funding and have been successful in increasing resources for students in low-wealth districts, they have been less successful in ensuring that these same students are able to access a high-quality education. Indeed, more school finance cases like *Yazzie/Martinez* are needed that push the school equity debate beyond just funding and also look at the quality of educational opportunities (Martin et al., 2018).

MONEY MAKES A DIFFERENCE IN EDUCATIONAL OPPORTUNITIES

Baker et al. (2018), in their review of recent research on the relationship between school funding and educational opportunity, found an overwhelming number of benefits, including:

- increased school funding leads to greater and more fairly distributed education resources;

- states that invest in the resources that matter—low pupil-to-teacher ratios, especially for high poverty districts, and competitive wages—tend to have higher academic outcomes among children from low-income families and smaller income-based achievement gaps;
- adequacy-oriented school funding reforms between 1990 and 2011 achieved their goals of improving educational opportunity by raising achievement among students in low-income districts;
- school funding reform also leads to improvements far beyond test scores: increased spending led to higher high school graduation rates, greater educational attainment, higher earnings and lower rates of poverty in adulthood.

(p. 1)

Jackson et al. (2016) also found that "improved access to resources can profoundly shape the life outcomes of economically disadvantaged children, and thereby significantly reduce the intergenerational transmission of poverty" (p. 212). Of course, in order for school funding to improve outcomes, it must be spent in effective ways to benefit those most in need.

Although we know the many benefits of school funding, such as the ones previously mentioned, and school finance litigation has helped in making progress around economic inequality in U.S., there are still a number of states that have yet to implement finance systems that meet the needs of all students and school funding inequities continue to permeate the education system. Funding itself continues to be unequal among states, ranging from close to $19,000 per student in New York to approximately $6,300 in Idaho (Baker et al., 2018). Moreover, how funding is distributed based on need varies across states with 17 states regressively funding districts in high need, 20 states remaining flat in their funding distribution with no significant differences between funding for high- and low-wealth districts, and only 11 states utilizing a progressive model providing high-need districts with more funding (Baker et al., 2018).

Some states have stepped in to compensate for the school-funding imbalance—Vermont and Hawaii (89% each) are the highest, while South Dakota (30%) and Illinois (24%) are the lowest in state school funding sources (McFarland et al., 2019). Yet, states like Vermont and Hawaii tend to be the exceptions as the public investment in schools continues to decline and local property wealth dictates the level of resources school districts have access to.

There are efforts being made by some states to try to remedy their current school funding levels. For instance, Illinois has long been the frontrunner as the state with the largest inequality in school funding in the U.S. (Morgan & Amerikaner, 2018). However, in summer 2017, the Illinois state legislature finally concluded a long battle over determining a more equitable school funding formula and came to a compromise on a school funding plan. The new school funding plan calculates the amount each district needs to provide an adequate, quality education, and then compares this amount to how much the district can reasonably raise in property taxes to reach the adequate funding threshold. More than half of the districts in the state are unable to raise even half of what they need to provide an adequate education, but 140 districts have more than 100% of the adequate funding they need due to plentiful property tax sources; some districts even have more than twice the adequate funding (Rhodes, 2018). Thus, with the new funding plan the state will funnel supplemental dollars to districts that are unable to meet this educational adequacy metric, and districts in the greatest need will receive more state dollars.

Although school funding experts see Illinois' new school funding policy as a step in the right direction to funding equalization, and in line with recommendations by scholars such as Darling-Hammond (2019), who encourages states to "focus funding on pupil needs and the costs of meeting the state's standards" as well as ensuring "flexibility to make locally appropriate, strategic decisions about how to spend resources to achieve results" (p. 24), the metric for this funding formula is adequacy and not equity, and thus may still be insufficient. As we discussed previously, only an adequacy rationale provides the minimum level of funding needed for every school to teach its students. However, due to the long history of policies and structures that denied students of color opportunities to a quality education, it would take more than minimum adequate funding to redress these inequities (Morgan & Amerikaner, 2018; see Rothstein, 2017). Therefore, school funding policies like Illinois are color-evasive because they prioritize a district's economic inequality and do not consider how a host of racial inequities like racial discrimination in housing, employment, and commerce are key factors contributing to district inequities in financial resources.

SCHOOL LEADERS ROLE IN SCHOOL FUNDING

Among the many responsibilities of a school leader is the ability to oversee school budgets and operations. And in recent years, schools have been given more autonomy when it comes to how they allocate their resources, which can be helpful in directing resources to specific priorities though may at the same time increase inequities between schools. Indeed, schools in low-wealth areas are less likely to be able to supplement money received from the state through parent organizations or other community contributions. Inequities can then be further perpetuated when we are unable to truly monitor the exact resources and revenues brought into schools, which include contributions at the local level, and so can make it difficult to design school funding systems that seek to achieve resource parity (OECD, 2017). In Standard 9 of the Professional Standards for Educational Leaders (PSEL, 2015)—Operations and Management—effective leaders are ones defined as, among other things, ethical stewards of their schools' monetary resources. Indeed, school leaders need to and are required to be transparent in their funding decisions.

School leaders also need to possess the capacity and support to make school funding decisions. By engaging in ongoing professional development on school finance, which includes being aware of how school funding is appropriated at the state and local levels, school leaders can be more effective in their decision-making around resources and make better decisions about how to equitably allocate money in their own schools (Leonardo & Grubb, 2014).

We also believe that if school leaders are interested in achieving equity in their schools, access and opportunity to material items (e.g., resources) and nonmaterial items (e.g., equity-minded curriculum, pedagogies, and teachers) must be redistributed (Gorski, 2019). Gorski argues, and we agree, that if we are committed to eradicating the way racism manifests itself in our schools, the interests of students of color must be prioritized in every decision around policy and practice, including the redistribution of access and educational opportunity. A school leader committed to racial equity must consistently advocate for stronger school investments and resources and take direct actions to ensure funding is allocated to reach those students most in need.

CONCLUSION

Recent teacher strikes across many states have brought to light challenges school districts face around funding. The battle over more equitable school funding is ongoing due in part to the narrow policy focus on simply reforming school funding formulas. Instead policy makers and educational administrators should collaborate to reform multiple, interconnected racially inequitable policies linked to inequities in school funding like housing discrimination, unemployment, and scarcity of commercial investments in communities of color (Rothstein, 2017). When states continue to fund public education in terms of adequacy instead of equity, and do not place access to quality education front and center, our field must be better equipped on all fronts to confront structures and systems that perpetuate educational inequity. We want educational leaders to place the role racism plays in school funding inequalities at the core of policy discussions in order to take action and avert the potential racial inequities school funding policies cause when implemented.

DISCUSSION QUESTIONS

1. What factors are included in your state's school funding formula? How does the formula work to close funding gaps and ensure all students are receiving a high-quality education?
2. What does funding per pupil look like in school districts across your state? How does your district compare to other districts?
3. How has school finance been litigated in your state and what are the outcomes?
4. What does the education clause in your state constitution include? Do you feel the language equitably and/or adequately addresses students' educational rights? How so?
5. What is your role as a leader in implementing policy and practices around fiscal equity?
6. As a leader, how do you prioritize expenditures in your school? How do you determine what expenditures are effective or futile? How does racial equity play a role in your decision-making?

SCHOOL FUNDING RESOURCES

- A Quick Glance at School Finance: A 50 State Survey of School Finance Policies: https://schoolfinancesdav.wordpress.com/
- Center on Budget and Policy Priorities: www.cbpp.org/
- Economic Policy Institute: www.epi.org
- EdBuild: https://edbuild.org/
- Education Law Center: https://edlawcenter.org

- The Education Trust: https://edtrust.org
- Equality of Opportunity and Education Project, Stanford University: https://edeq.stanford.edu/
- Learning Policy Institute: https://learningpolicyinstitute.org
- NPR Series School Money: The Cost of Opportunity: www.npr.org/series/473636949/schoolmoney
- SchoolFunding.Info: A Project of the Center for Educational Equity at Teachers College: http://schoolfunding.info/

RECOMMENDED READINGS

Baker, B. D. (2017). *How money matters for schools.* Palo Alto, CA: Learning Policy Institute.

Carter, P. L., & Welner, K. G. (2013). *Closing the opportunity gap: What America must do to give every child an even chance.* New York: Oxford University Press.

Darling-Hammond, L. (2019). *Investing for student success: Lessons from state school finance reforms.* Palo Alto, CA: Learning Policy Institute.

Rice, J. K. (2015). *Investing in equal opportunity: What would it take to build the balance wheel?.* Boulder, CO: National Education Policy Center.

REFERENCES

Abbott v. Burke, 100 N.J. 269, 495 A.2d 376 (1985).

Baker, B. D., Farrie, D., & Sciarra, D. (2018). *Is school funding fair? A national report card* (7th edition). Newark, NJ: Education Law Center.

Burnette, II, D. (2019a). Breaking down the where & why of K-12 spending. *Education Week, 39*(6), 12–17.

Burnette, II, D. (2019b). Educators' money jitters never far below surface. *Education Week, 39*(6), 3–4.

California Department of Education. (2019). *Local control funding formula overview.* Retrieved from www.cde.ca.gov/fg/aa/lc/lcffoverview.asp

Campaign for Fiscal Equity Inc. v. State of New York et al., 100 N.Y.2d 893 (2003).

Darling-Hammond, L. (2019). *Investing for student success: Lessons from state school finance reforms.* Palo Alto, CA: Learning Policy Institute.

Disare, M. (2018, March 29). Here's the education lawsuit that helped motivate Cynthia Nixon's run for governor. *Chalkbeat.* Retrieved from www.chalkbeat.org/posts/ny/2018/03/29/heres-the-education-lawsuit-that-helped-motivate-cynthia-nixons-run-for-governor/

EdBuild. (2019). *$23 billion.* Jersey City, NJ: Author. Retrieved from https://edbuild.org/content/23-billion/full-report.pdf

Edgewood Independent School District v. Kirby 777 S.W.2d. 391 (Tex. 1989).

Education Law Center. (2019). *State profiles*. Retrieved from https://edlawcenter.org/states

Education Week Research Center. (2019). We asked about school finance. What did districts say? *Education Week, 39*(6), 5–8.

Farrie, D., Kim, R., & Sciarra, D.G. (2019). *Making the grade 2019: How fair is school funding in your state?* Newark, NJ: Education Law Center.

Gorski, P. (2019). Avoiding racial equity detours. *Educational Leadership, 76*(7), 56–61.

Green, P. C., Baker, B. D., & Oluwole, J. O. (2008). Race-conscious funding strategies and school finance litigation. *Boston University Public Interest Law Journal, 16*, 39–71.

Hinojosa, D. G. (2016). "Race-conscious" school finance litigation: Is a fourth wave emerging? *University of Richmond Law Review, 50*, 869–892.

Jackson, C. K., Johnson, R. C., & Persico, C. (2016). The effects of school spending on educational and economic outcomes: Evidence from school finance reforms. *The Quarterly Journal of Economics*, 131(1), 157–218.

Johnson, R. C., & Tanner, S. (2018). *Money and freedom: The impact of California's school finance reform on academic achievement and the composition of district spending*. Palo Alto, CA: Learning Policy Institute.

Lafortune, J., Rothstein, J., & Schanzenbach, D. W. (2016). *Can school finance reforms improve student achievement?* Washington, D.C.: The Washington Center for Equitable Growth.

Leachman, M. (2019). *K-12 funding still lagging in many states*. Washington, D.C.: Center on Budget and Priorities. Retrieved from www.cbpp.org/blog/k-12-funding-still-lagging-in-many-states

Leachman, M., & Figueroa, E. (2019). *K-12 school funding up in most 2018 teacher-protest states, but still well below decade ago*. Washington, D.C.: Center on Budget and Priorities. Retrieved from www.cbpp.org/sites/default/files/atoms/files/3-6-19sfp.pdf

Leonardo, Z., & Norton, G.W. (2014). *Education and racism: A primer on issues and dilemmas*. New York: Routledge.

Martin, C., Boser, U., Benner, M., & Baffour, P. (2018). *A quality approach to school funding*. Washington, D.C.: Center for American Progress. Retrieved from www.americanprogress.org/issues/education-k-12/reports/2018/11/13/460397/quality-approach-school-funding/

McFarland, J., Hussar, B., Zhang, J., Wang, X., Wang, K., Hein, S., Diliberti, M., Forrest Cataldi, E., Bullock Mann, F., & Barmer, A. (2019). *The Condition of Education 2019 (NCES 2019-144)*. Washington, D.C.: National Center for Education Statistics. Retrieved from https://nces.ed.gov/pubsearch/pubsinfo.asp?pubid=2019144

Morath v. Texas Taxpayer & Student Fairness Coalition, 490 S.W.3d 826, 833 (Tex. 2016).

Morgan, I., & Amerikaner, A. (2018, February). *Funding gaps: An analysis of school funding equity across the U.S. and within each state*. Washington D.C.: Education Trust. Retrieved from https://edtrust.org/resource/funding-gaps-2018/

National Policy Board for Educational Administration. (2015). *Professional standards for Educational Leaders 2015*. Reston, VA: Author.

New Mexico Center on Law and Poverty. (2018). *Yazzie/Martinez v. State of New Mexico decision*. Albuquerque, NM: Author. Retrieved from http://nmpovertylaw.org/wp-content/uploads/2018/09/Graphic-Yazzie-Martinez-Decision.pdf

Organisation for Economic Co-operation and Development. (2017). *The funding of school education: Connecting resources and learning*. Paris, France: OECD Publishing. Retrieved from www.oecd-ilibrary.org

Rebell, M. A. (2017). The courts' consensus: Money does matter for educational opportunity. *The ANNALS of the American Academy of Political and Social Science, 674*, 184–198.

Rhodes, D. (2018, April 6). Equity dollars set to go to schools. *NPR Illinois*. Retrieved from http://nprillinois.org/post/equity-dollars-set-go-schools#stream/0

Rose v. Council for Better Education, 790 S.W.2d 186, (Ky. 1989).

Rothstein, R. (2017). *The color of law: A forgotten history of how our government segregated America*. New York: Liveright Publishing Co.

Ryan, J. E. (1999). The influence of race in school finance reform. *Michigan Law Review, 98*(2), 432–481.

San Antonio Independent School District v. Rodriguez, 411 U.S. 1 (1973).

Serrano v. Priest, 5 Cal.3d 584 (1971).

Swaby, A., & Ura, A. (2018, December 12). Texas has failed to close educational gaps for kids of color. In Edgewood ISD, the fallout has lasted generations. *The Texas Tribune*. Retrieved from www.texastribune.org/2018/12/18/edgewood-isd-neglect-texas-public-students-of-color/

The Texas Politics Project. (n.d.). *Edgewood ISD v. Kirby*. Austin, TX: The University of Texas at Austin. Retrieved from https://texaspolitics.utexas.edu/educational-resources/edgewood-isd-v-kirby

Yazzie/Martinez v. New Mexico, No. D-101-CV-2014-00793, No. D-101-CV-2014–02224 (1st Dis. New Mexico, 2018).

Chapter 7

Racism and School Discipline
From Schools to Prison, or Schools *As* a Prison

Michelle Alexander's (2010) book *The New Jim Crow: Mass Incarceration in the Era of Colorblindness*, first published 10 years ago, unmasked how the prison industrial complex has become a modern racial caste system that disproportionately affects Black and Brown families. The system of Jim Crow legally ended when President Lyndon B. Johnson signed the 1964 Civil Rights Act, but in her book Alexander explains how the current web of legal and policy channels that may on the surface seem non-racial is very much an intentional form of white supremacy and modern-day slavery that is hidden in plain sight. She contends that we as a society have decided that those who are deemed criminal should be out of sight, out of mind, and undeserving of humanity. Moreover, the prison industrial complex is also neoliberal as public and private entities conspire to mastermind how prisons can serve to make profit. Like most neoliberal structures, the prison industrial complex is not partisan as both Republican and Democratic political decisions are responsible for its construction (Alexander, 2010). Ronald Reagan's War on Drugs, Bill Clinton's "three strikes" law, and Barack Obama funneling billions of dollars from the 2009 stimulus package to support state and local law enforcement in fighting drug crime are all policies that furthered the policing and exponential imprisonment of Black and Brown people (Alexander, 2010).

However, the criminal "justice" system and all its political and legal complexities is not the only system that fuels the prison industrial complex, as PK-12 education is part of the problem as well. Black students, specifically, are disproportionately disciplined more than any racial or ethnic group, and this racial injustice begins as early as preschool. For instance, in the 2013–14 school year, Black students only represented about 19.5% of preschoolers but 46% were suspended once and 48% more than once, whereas white students represented 42% of preschoolers that year but only 28% were suspended once and 27% more than once (U.S. Department of Education, 2014). Black students are more frequently and harshly disciplined not because they act out more or engage in more severe behaviors than other peer groups, but unfortunately because schools largely view them through a deficit lens (Rudd, 2014). Moreover, with every disciplinary infraction a student receives, the probability of them being a product of the criminal justice system at some point increases, a phenomenon now widely known as the *school-to-prison pipeline*.

According to the U.S. Commission on Civil Rights (2019), the "prison track" or the "school-to-prison pipeline" refers to

> how education policies implemented over the past several decades have worked to remove students from schools and funnel them onto a one-way path toward prison. Behavior that once led to a trip to the principal's office and detention, such as school uniform violations, profanity and "talking back," now often leads to suspension, expulsion, and/or arrest.
>
> (p. 38)

In their review of the research, Skiba, Arredondo, and Williams (2017) identified four common themes on how the research problematizes the school-to-prison pipeline: (1) exclusionary forms of discipline such as out-of-school suspensions and expulsions have become "widespread, systematic, and increasing" in usage; (2) the severity with which exclusionary discipline policies and practices are implemented in public schools not only decreases young people's chances of experiencing success in school but also increases the likelihood they will encounter negative life outcomes, especially involvement with the juvenile justice system; (3) exclusionary disciplinary practices and the resultant outcomes disproportionately impact students of color; and (4) the construct "school-to-prison pipeline" suggests that it is the school's policies and practices and not simply students' characteristics that are to some extent responsible for these negative outcomes (p. 113).

There is not a direct, linear path from school to justice system involvement. A variety of factors drive the school-to-prison pipeline (Skiba et al., 2017). Schools with a negative culture and climate have higher incidents of exclusionary discipline practices, and so school culture and climate matter to educators' disciplinary practices (Skiba et al., 2017). For example, Mattison and Aber (2007) found that Black high school students had more negative perceptions of their schools' racial climate as compared to their white peers, and their experiences with racism was associated with getting lower grades and more detentions and suspensions than their white peers. Therefore, students' of color experiences with racism negatively affect their overall learning opportunities, academic achievement, and level of engagement in school. Also, when a disciplinary consequence is used to remove the student from the educational setting the student is essentially excluded from and denied learning opportunities. This loss of instructional time due to exclusionary discipline is not only tied to poor achievement outcomes, but also hurts the student's ability to form positive relationships with teachers and school administrators causing the student to be disengaged from school (Lewis, Butler, Bonner, & Joubert, 2010; McNeely, Nonemaker, & Blum, 2002). Repeated suspensions further disengage students from school and increase the likelihood they will drop out (Fabelo, Thompson, Plompkin, Carmichael, Marchbanks, & Booth, 2011). Thus, instead of waiting for a student to drop out of their own accord, repeated suspensions are a mechanism in which a school can push a student out (NCSSD, n.d.). The justice system is the final stop in the school-to-prison pipeline. Even as early as third grade, students who receive one or two suspensions are eight times as likely to be placed in alternative schools and students who receive three or more suspensions are 25 times as likely (Vanderhaar, Petrosko, & Munoz, 2015). Getting suspended in middle school or high school also triples a student's likelihood of juvenile justice contact the following year (Fabelo et al., 2011).

The alarming rate at which students of color are harshly disciplined has been on the educational policy radar for some time now, with even some state and local reform efforts being implemented to redress these racist practices (Rafa, 2019). Nevertheless, this increased awareness of the problem has not improved the lived realities of students of color as they still have a higher probability of being a victim of *exclusionary disciplinary* practices. For example, in the 2015–16 school year, which is the most recent data available, Black male and female students each represented approximately 8% of all public school students, but were 25% and 14% of students respectively who were suspended out of school, while white students across both genders were underrepresented (U.S. Department of Education Office of Civil Rights, 2018). Nationally, Black students are a victim of exclusionary discipline more so than any racial or ethnic group, and it is important to extend beyond the

Black–white paradigm and explore how context matters to who is on the receiving end of more discipline practices. In Wyoming, for example, disproportionate suspensions are highest among Native American and Latinx students. For female Native American students, there is a +5.5 percentage point difference between their rate of enrollment and percent of all suspensions, and a +5.6 percentage point difference for male Native American students. Latinx students have a +3.8 percentage point difference between their rate of enrollment and percent of all suspensions, and a +3.9 percentage point difference for Latinx male students. Yet, white students are significantly underrepresented for discipline referrals with white females at a −12.5 percentage point difference between their rate of enrollment and percent of all suspensions, and white males at a −12.7 percentage point difference.

Exclusionary discipline is any form of disciplinary practice that results in removing or excluding a student from their typical educational setting (NCSSD, n.d.). Exclusionary disciplinary practices include in-school suspensions where students are removed from class but still supervised, out-of-school suspensions where a student is temporarily removed from their school for at least half a day, and expulsion that removes a student for the remainder of the school year with or without any educational instruction (U.S. Department of Education, n.d.). Moreover, for many students policing in school has become the disciplinary norm, and some urban school districts like Baltimore City Public Schools (Maryland) and Austin Independent School District (Texas) have their own police forces. For students of color, school is not only a potential pipeline to prison, but school can already feel like a prison. In this chapter, we further examine the racial implications of exclusionary discipline practices, focusing on two policy issues: (1) zero tolerance policies and (2) the role of policing and criminalization of students of color in school. We then discuss how strategies like Response to Intervention (RTI) and Positive Behavior Intervention Supports (PBIS), while intended to be a more humane alternative to exclusionary discipline practice, may instead maintain white norms for student behavior. Finally, we make recommendations for more antiracist alternatives to exclusionary discipline practices.

ZERO TOLERANCE POLICIES

Ostensibly, exclusionary discipline practices should be used as a last resort consequence for objective, rule-based violations like bringing a weapon to school. Unfortunately, under a *zero tolerance policy* exclusionary discipline can be used as a catchall consequence for even minor infractions. Zero tolerance is a "one-size-fits-all" approach to discipline that enables school leaders to deliver extremely punitive consequences regardless of what end of the spectrum the student's behavior falls, from being tardy to class to bringing a weapon onto school property (U.S. Commission on Civil Rights, 2019, p. 27).

Zero tolerance policies originated from the federal Gun-Free School Act of 1994, which at the time was a policy response to the growing concern about the supposed increase in juvenile crime in the 1980s (U.S. Commission on Civil Rights, 2019). Then, in compliance with the Gun-Free School Act, local education agencies adopted policies that required educators to issue expulsions to students found in possession of firearms on campus (U.S. Commission on Civil Rights, 2019). The 1999 Columbine High School shooting further precipitated a fear of gun violence in schools, and from that tragic day until the early 2000s there was an increase in the implementation of zero tolerance policies to ensure school safety (Rafa, 2019; U.S. Commission of Civil Rights, 2019). However, many states soon overcorrected and implemented exclusionary discipline policies that were even more stringent than the original federal mandate (U.S. Commission on Civil Rights, 2019).

Undeniably, since Columbine there have been several high-profile school shootings, and we still are in desperate need of policy reforms that address the root cause of the nation's fixation with guns and gun violence. Surprisingly though, the rates of school violence are actually not as extreme as the policy discourse has made it out to be, and instead have remained steady over the last several decades. However, fear often drives policy decisions, as zero tolerance policies have done little to decrease incidents of school violence (U.S. Commission on Civil Rights, 2019).

While zero tolerance policies were originally intended to address violent infractions, in practice educators use this approach primarily as a consequence for non-violent, minor infractions, which are behaviors that educators *subjectively* view as disruptive (Duncan, 2014; U.S. Commission on Civil Rights, 2019). In a state level study, Rausch and Skiba (2006) found that only 5% of out-of-school suspensions were actually for serious infractions like drugs or weapons, while 95% of suspensions were for disruptive or other behaviors. Thus, zero tolerance policies have not had the desired effect that they were originally intended to.

Considering the extent to which zero tolerance policies disproportionately exclude students of color from learning opportunities, several states have decided to roll back exclusionary discipline policies like suspension and expulsion and instead implement policies that are less punitive and promote a positive school culture and climate (Rafa, 2019). According to an Education Commission of the States policy brief, in the last five years state legislatures have only passed seven bills that support suspension and expulsion (Rafa, 2019), whereas, 36 bills were passed that impeded the use of suspension and expulsion and instead promoted alternative and less-punitive discipline approaches (Rafa, 2019). Disaggregating data by race is important to directly naming the problem of racial disproportionality of school discipline. Currently, at least 33 states and the District of Columbia require some form of reporting on school discipline, and 11 states and the District of Columbia require suspensions and expulsion data be disaggregated by demographic subgroups like race, gender, and disability status.

EDUCATORS DON'T "TREAT ALL STUDENTS THE SAME": RACE AND THE SEVERITY OF THE INFRACTION

A common color-evasive defense mechanism white people use to not appear racist is to affirm that "I treat everyone the same because I don't see color" (Bonilla-Silva, 2017; DiAngelo, 2018). However, when it comes to school discipline, this mantra of white fragility could not be further from the truth, as educators do not treat all students the same when issuing disciplinary consequences. Not only are students of color disciplined more than white students, if a white student and a student of color commit the same infraction it is highly likely that the student of color would receive the harsher consequence, and society reinforces this unfairness. If a white person and person of color are charged with the same crime, the person of color is likely to receive a harsher punishment—as evident in recent murders of Black youth, including Trayvon Martin, Michael Brown, and Laquan McDonald, to name a few, by white police officers (see Alexander, 2010).

There are distinct racial differences among students in the severity of disciplinary infractions. For example, a Texas study found that Black students were more likely than white or Latinx students to be disciplined for discretionary offenses like tardiness, leaving class early, or dress code violations. Similarly, when examining discipline data in Arkansas K-12 schools over a seven-year period (2008–09 to 2014–15), Anderson and Ritter (2017) found that 80% of the discipline referrals were for minor non-violent offenses like disorderly conduct and insubordination. Also, Black students received harsher exclusionary punishments for these minor offenses. Black students were almost 2.5 times more likely to receive exclusionary discipline than their white peers in the same grade for the same type of infraction. Likewise, low-income students were 1.5 times more likely than their more affluent peers to receive exclusionary discipline for the same type of infraction. Schools with a higher percentage of students of color, more specifically Black students, issued harsher and longer punishments. Interestingly, open enrollment charter schools in the state gave harsher punishments as well. Charter schools in Arkansas are primarily located in urban areas and have higher percentages of Black students compared to white students. The researchers attributed this finding to charter school networks like the Knowledge is Power Program (KIPP) that adhere to a "no excuses" approach to discipline. Finally, even when controlling for poverty levels of the school, ultimately race matters most to discipline disproportionality. Students in higher-income, nonwhite schools received an extra half-day of discipline for every infraction, compared to students in predominately white, higher-income schools. Also, students in low-income, nonwhite schools received 0.6 extra days of punishment compared to students in white, low-income schools.

Racial disproportionality of school discipline is also linked to school segregation, a policy issue previously discussed in Chapters 2 and 3 of this book. Upon examining statewide data in Indiana, Gopalan and Nelson (2019) found that 82% of Black students attended the 35 districts (out of 400) that accounted for 51% of the suspensions and expulsions in the state, but Black students only represent 38% of student enrollment. One explanation for this finding is that Black students are overwhelmingly segregated in districts with "punitive disciplinary environments" (p.13). According to the researchers, if Black students in Indiana were "re-sorted" and attended predominately white schools situated in districts that had lower than average disciplinary rates, "the Black-White disciplinary gap would decline by 11% to 25% across grade levels" (p. 14). Gopalan and Nelson infer that,

> The uneven distribution of Black students across districts likely corresponds to the uneven distribution of resources, teacher quality, and other factors that are associated with adverse disciplinary outcomes... also minority students who attend schools with more minority (or poor) students exhibit similar behaviors but are treated differently. For example, schools with more minority and poor students may experience a larger presence of school resource officers, which may increase the likelihood of punitive disciplinary action conditional on behavior.
>
> (p. 14)

POLICING IN SCHOOLS

Zero tolerance policies are on the decline now that there is a greater awareness of how these policies contribute to the school-to-prison pipeline. However, the ways in which schools can feel like prisons still endures, as policing in schools remains through other reform efforts and policies. And while zero-tolerance policies came to the fore in response to the 1999 Columbine school shooting 20 years ago, unfortunately history has repeated itself with a number of recent high-profile school shootings. CNN reported that in the first 21 weeks of 2018 there were 23 school shootings where someone was killed or injured, with the most highly profiled being the shooting on February 14 of that year at Marjory Stoneman Douglas High School in Parkland, Florida (Ahmed & Walker, 2018). Yet, school shootings account for less than 3% of youth homicides, and so fear largely clouds school and district communities' decisions about policing and school safety (Keierleber, 2019).

Nevertheless, driven by fear in response to these more recent school shootings many school communities across the country are still considering increasing the level of policing in schools as a solution (Barnum, 2019). For example, Manor Independent School District, a district with a majority student of color enrollment (66.7% Latinx, 22.8% Black) on the northeast side of Austin, Texas, recently decided to create its own police department based on neoliberal terms. Essentially, the district having its own police department was described as a more economical option than to rely on the city's policy department. The assistant superintendent explained, "We're thrilled that we're going to be able to provide even more of a police presence and security for our students at a lower price than we're currently paying now" (Vidal, 2019, par. 1). However, the possible racial implications of ramping up police presence in a district that serves primarily Brown and Black students was absent from this discussion.

Based on the most recent 2015–16 Civil Rights Data Collection (CRDC), 1.6 million students attend school with sworn law enforcement but do not have any school counselors. That same school year, there were more school resource officers (SROs) (27,000) than social workers (23,000) in U.S. public schools (U.S. Commission on Civil Rights, 2019). Likewise, an investigation into the 10 largest school districts in the U.S. found that four of the school districts—Chicago, Houston, New York City, and Miami-Dade—had more school police officers than school counselors (Barnum, 2016; U.S. Commission on Civil Rights, 2019). Also, students' contact with school law enforcement increases with every school level (Lindsay, Lee, & Lloyd, 2018).

Approximately 67% of high school students, 45% of middle school students, and 19% of elementary school students attend schools with a police officer (Lindsay et al., 2018). There are also regional differences in the level of policing in schools. Southern and mid-Atlantic states have the highest level of policing. In states such as Florida, Maryland, North Carolina, South Carolina, Tennessee, and Virginia, 90% or more of high school students attend a school that has a police officer.

Youth are now exposed to police officers in school more than any other support services important to their academic success. And there are individuals who endorse this heavy police presence and what they believe to be the benefits of having police in schools. Advocates believe that police presence in schools creates a safe space for students to learn by warding off any violent student behaviors and crime, and also see it as an opportunity to build bridges between the police, school, and the community (Corley, 2018; Lindsay et al., 2018). However, there is very little research that demonstrates the effectiveness of law enforcement in schools, and of the research that does exist, the methodological rigor is questionable (Lindsay et al., 2018; U.S. Commission on Civil Rights, 2019). Instead, the presence of law enforcement in schools criminalizes even normal adolescent misbehavior and minor offenses, increases the number of student arrests, and is linked to increases in student referrals to the justice system (Lindsay et al., 2018; Petteruti, 2011; Theriot, 2009). For example, using data from the School Survey on Crime and Safety one study found that as schools increase their use of police, they record more weapons and drug offenses and also report a higher percentage of non-serious crimes to law enforcement (Na & Gottfredson, 2013). Another study was conducted in a single southeastern school district that compared schools *with* SROs, which are local law enforcement assigned to a school, to schools *without* and came up with similar findings. When controlling for school socioeconomic status the presence of a SRO increased the likelihood of a student arrest at a rate of 197.7% per 100 students. Also, with and without controlling for poverty, the presence of a SRO increased the likelihood a student would be arrested for disorderly conduct at a rate of 402.3% per 100 students and 128.2% per 100 students, respectively (Theriot, 2009).

Policing as Racial Violence in Schools

Back in late October 2015, several videos taken from students' cell phones of a white South Carolina police officer violently disciplining a Black female student for being disruptive in class went viral. In the videos, the police officer tells the student that she needs to leave her seat or he will forcibly remove her. Then, the officer proceeds to wrap his arm around her neck, which then results in the student's desk flipping backwards to the ground. The officer then proceeds to drag the student to the front of the classroom to handcuff her in front of her peers. At the time of the incident, the public was outraged over what they saw in the videos and the officer was subsequently fired from his job. The media attention this video received made it impossible to ignore the link between racism and policing in schools, and sparked more public conversation on the issue of the physical and psychological violence and humiliation students of color experience when they are arrested in front of their peers (see Fausset, Pérez-Peña, & Blinder, 2015). Unfortunately, the racial violence in this video is not an isolated incident as there are numerous examples covered by the news, and even in the research, where students of color voice their experiences of being arrested by police in school, such as getting slammed against tables and walls while handcuffed, being fingerprinted, and even getting their mugshots taken (Corley, 2018).

Based on the 2015–16 Civil Rights Data Collection (U.S. Department of Education, 2018), Black students only represented 15% of overall student enrollment, but 31% of students arrested at school or referred to law enforcement. Thus, Black students are twice as likely as white students to be referred to law enforcement or arrested in school (U.S. GAO, 2018). Native Hawaiian or other Pacific Islander students are the only other racial or ethnic subgroup nationally with a slight school discipline disproportionality, representing 0.4 % of overall enrollment, but 1% of all students arrested at school. Similarly, Finn and Servoss (2014) found that Black students were more likely to be enrolled in schools that used high levels of security. Moreover, Black students that attend schools with high levels of security and policing, when controlling for students' misbehavior and school characteristics, were twice (odds ratio = 2.3) as likely as white students to be suspended. Furthermore, Black students had the highest suspension rates out of any racial or ethnic group. However, the differences between suspensions of Black and white students in low security schools was not statistically significant even when controlling or not controlling for student misbehavior. These findings suggest that schools with lower levels of policing and surveillance perhaps treat Black students more equitably.

Furthermore, educators' racial biases can negatively influence their assessment of students' of color misbehaviors. Using a sample of children born between 1998 and 2000 in 20 U.S. cities with populations over 200,000, Owens and McLanahan (2019) found that racial differences in behavior represented only a small fraction of disparity in discipline. However, it was teachers' differential treatment of Black and white students that made up 46% of the racial gap in suspension and expulsions for five- to nine-year-old students. In contrast, 21% of the racial gap could be explained by the difference in the school characteristics that Black and white students primarily attend, and differences in student behavior comprised only 9% of the racial gap. As one of the researchers, Jayani Owens, explained in an interview highlighting the study's findings:

> Not only were Black children more likely to be suspended, but these racial differences were happening in the same schools...It shows that the categories that teachers use for punishment, like "defiance", "disrespect" and "noncompliance" are ripe for racial discrimination. What does it mean to be disrespectful? It would be easy for a teacher to read the behavior of a kid as disrespectful when it may not have been intended that way...The idea that you can have two kids of different races misbehaving in similar ways and receiving different forms of punishment—one gets a slap on the wrist, say, and the other gets suspended—is a really important thing to understand socially...Subconsciously, we all have racial biases in different ways. This is one way in which those biases are manifesting in the classroom.
> (The Journal of Blacks in Higher Education, 2019, par. 4–5)

Indeed, educators are not race-neutral—their racial biases weigh heavily on how they treat students of color.

INTERVENTIONS AND STRATEGIES THAT MAINTAIN WHITE BEHAVIORAL NORMS IN SCHOOLING

Currently, most states are moving away from exclusionary discipline practices and instead are using alternative approaches to school discipline. Thirty states and the District of Columbia encourage districts to use alternative school discipline strategies, and 22 of these states reference specific interventions (Rafa, 2018). Instead of excluding students from the learning environment as the default consequence for their misbehavior, alternative school discipline strategies encourage educators to find the root cause of a student's misbehavior and then address it by both repairing and building stronger relationships with the student and improving the student's overall engagement in learning (Rafa, 2019).

The federal government continues to endorse alternative school discipline strategies through policy and funding for states, districts, and schools. In 2014, the U.S. Department of Education and Department of Justice collaborated on the *Rethinking Discipline* campaign to address the overuse of exclusionary discipline practices like suspensions and expulsions. *Rethinking Discipline* also provided states with guidance on how to implement alternatives to exclusionary discipline, reduce bias and discriminatory practices, and identify the root causes of racial disproportionality in school discipline (U.S. GAO, 2018).

Also, both the U.S. Departments of Education and Justice sponsor grant programs that promote alternatives to exclusionary discipline. From 2014–16, the U.S Department of Education awarded $130 million to states and school districts through the School Climate Transformation Grant, and 3,000 schools used this grant program to implement behavioral supports. Based on preliminary data from this grant program, participating schools have increased student attendance and now have fewer disciplinary referrals (U.S. GAO, 2018). The second U.S. Department of Education grant, Project Prevent, awarded $68 million to 20 school districts between 2015 and 2019. Project Prevent encourages districts to develop students' conflict resolution skills, especially students who have been exposed to violence (U.S. GAO, 2018). School districts participating in Project Prevent provide mental health services to over 5,000 students and have 10,000 fewer violent behavioral incidents (U.S. GAO, 2018). Likewise, in 2014 the National Institute of Justice, a segment of the U.S. Department of Justice, launched the Comprehensive School Safety Initiative which provided $84 million to fund research projects that identify the root causes of the school-to-prison pipeline and develop interventions as alternatives to exclusionary discipline practices (U.S. GAO, 2018).

The most common alternatives to exclusionary discipline practices are response to intervention, positive behavioral interventions and supports, social emotional learning, restorative discipline, and trauma-informed practices. *Response to intervention* (RTI) is a multi-tiered, early identification and support system for students with learning and behavioral needs (RTI Action Network, n.d.). Instead of a wait to fail model, RTI aims to intervene early on in students' schooling (Fuchs, Mock, Morgan, & Young, 2003).

Like RTI, *Positive Behavior Interventions and Supports* (PBIS) is a multi-tiered framework that addresses positive student behavioral expectations through whole-system change. Evidence-based approaches are implemented at a schoolwide level to improve student behavior by teaching them "appropriate behaviors" (Rafa, 2019, p. 3) or essentially "what to do instead of what not to do" (U.S. GAO, 2018, p. 28). PBIS aims to change the school culture and climate by setting expectations for student behavior, establishing a continuum of behaviors and consequences, and then reinforcing positive student behaviors (Steinberg & Lacoe, 2017). *Social emotional learning* (SEL) is also a schoolwide model that develops students' self-awareness, self-control, and interpersonal skills so that they can then cope with everyday challenges. The general theory of action of SEL programs like Second Step or the Collaborative for Academic, Social, and Emotional Learning (CASEL) framework is that if students learn to problem-solve, self-discipline, and develop impulse control they are better primed for classroom learning (Committee for Children, n.d.)

Restorative discipline, also known as restorative justice, is a conflict resolution process borrowed from the criminal justice system. Restorative discipline attempts to build healthier relationships between educators and students, minimize and prevent harmful behavior, repair any harm done because of the behavior, engage in conflict resolution, hold students accountable for their behavior, and then address and discuss the needs of the community (The Advancement Project, 2014). Hence, through conflict resolution an individual student takes responsibility for their behavior and attempts to repair the damage done to the person they have wronged (The Advancement Project, 2014; Milner et al., 2019). Finally, *trauma-informed practices* create a schooling environment that considers the whole child, especially how a child's experience of stress and trauma impedes their learning and behaviors (NCTSN, 2017). Trauma-informed schools integrate support services from the school community, mental health agencies, and other community advocacy organizations to support the social, emotional, and academic needs of the child.

Yet, most of these aforementioned alternatives to exclusionary discipline are assimilative and expect students to adjust their behaviors to the school's cultural norms, but do not require the school to adjust to meet the social, emotional, and cultural needs of students (Welsh & Little, 2018). PBIS teaches students the "right way to behave", RTI "intervenes" to improve student behavior, and SEL builds student capacity to have better "self-control", and responsive discipline "repairs" student behaviors. Therefore, these interventions and strategies try to manage student behavior through "conformity" but do not address educators' racial biases or the cultural mismatch that exist between teachers and students of color (Welsh & Little, 2018, p. 773).

The original impetus for these alternatives was not just to reduce exclusionary discipline practices but to also redress the racial disproportionality of school discipline. While these alternatives have reduced the number of suspensions, they have not mitigated racial disparities in discipline. Instead, these alternatives to exclusionary discipline avoid addressing racism altogether (Mansfield, Rainbolt, & Fowler, 2018; Skiba, 2015; Welsh & Little, 2018). Consequently, the color-evasive manner in which alternatives to exclusionary discipline are designed and implemented unburdens educators from doing the hard work necessary to change their disciplinary practices, especially their racial biases. Instead, the onus is on students of color to remedy their own racial oppression by adapting to and adopting dominant norms for what it means to be a good, well-behaved student.

Since the U.S. educator force is predominately white, under a color-evasive approach to improving school culture, climate, and classroom management, students of color have to conform to white cultural norms to lower their risk of falling victim to exclusionary discipline practices. Educators' racial biases and differential treatment of students of color largely explain the racial disparities in exclusionary discipline (Owens and McLanahan, 2019) and so any interventions and strategies that serve as an alternative to exclusionary practices are futile if they do not push educators to critically examine how their racial biases and disciplinary practices may contribute to the school-to-prison pipeline.

ANTI-RACIST APPROACHES AND RECOMMENDATIONS FOR EDUCATIONAL LEADERS

The current policies, interventions, strategies, and other trends that attempt to veer educators away from using exclusionary discipline may have successfully lowered suspension and expulsion rates, but unfortunately these solutions do so by catering to whiteness. These alternatives to exclusionary discipline make educators feel like they are doing something to address the problem while still protecting them from admitting the role they play in perpetuating racial inequities in discipline in the first place, and prevent them from changing the racist structure itself. Thus, interventions and strategies like RTI, PBIS, SEL are race-neutral in their design and implementation and permit educators to pretend to be addressing racial inequality without appearing racist. In conclusion, we provide recommendations for how educational leaders can help their districts and school communities name the root cause of racial disparities in school discipline—school-sponsored racism. Until we as educators acknowledge how we are a part of the problem of racism and discipline, any racial disparities that exist will continue to go unresolved.

Promote Youth Voice in Educational Policy and Practice

Young people are often more willing to speak out against racial injustices than adults, especially if school personnel feel their hands are tied by district bureaucracy or if they fear the backlash of publicly redressing racism in schools (Welton, Harris, Altamirano, & Williams, 2017). Young people also have a long history of igniting racial justice movements in education, whether it is through conducting youth participatory action research (YPAR) on school and societal problems that matter most to them and then finding their solutions, or using youth community organizing and activist tactics to achieve policy changes that lead to racial justice for young people (Welton & Bertrand, 2019; Welton et al., 2017). For example, for three years Welton and colleagues (2017) collaborated with a high school teacher and students in a social justice elective class where students used YPAR to uncover institutional racism in their school. One subtopic the students explored was race, school discipline, and the school-to-prison pipeline. At the time the high school administration did not disaggregate their discipline data by race. For several months the students in the social justice class conducted ethnographic observations of the in-school suspension (ISS) room and found that Black students made up the majority of students repeatedly in ISS and as a result were losing significant instructional time. The students presented their research findings to the school administration and the school decided to change their school procedures by mandating that school discipline data be disaggregated by race.

Illinois is one of few states in the nation with a statewide law, S.B. 100, that prohibits zero tolerance policies and requires districts and schools to implement alternatives to exclusionary discipline. VOYCE (Voices of Youth in Chicago Education) led the efforts to write and both pass S.B. 100. VOYCE is a youth grassroots community organizing group in Chicago primarily made up of high school students. The youth community organizing group originally crafted the bill in 2012 to address the impact of out-of-school suspensions and expulsions on students of color in Illinois. Members of VOYCE spent two years doing the groundwork and regularly traveling to the state capital in Springfield, Illinois, to educate their legislators on racial disproportionality in school discipline in the state, and the school-to-prison pipeline (Sanchez, 2015). Since S.B. 100 became law, and now that all districts and schools in Illinois are required to implement alternatives to exclusionary discipline, the number of suspensions and expulsions in the state has significantly decreased. Between 2011–12 and 2015–16 the state of Illinois' out-of-school suspension rate decreased from 6.1% to 3.4% (The Council of State Governments Justice Center, 2017).

Hire More Educators of Color

Educators of color generally have higher expectations of and hold students of color to a higher standard than white educators (Gilliam, Maupin, Reyes, Accavitti, & Shic, 2016). Gershenson, Holt, and Papageorge (2016) found that Black teachers had 30% to 40% higher expectations of Black students than non-Black teachers. Moreover, teachers have more empathy for a misbehaving student if the student and teachers' race are the same. In this same study, it was found that when there was a mismatch between the teacher and students' racial identity, the teacher then viewed the students' behavior to be difficult to address (Gilliam et al., 2016). This data shows that for students of color having a teacher whose identity matches their own racial and cultural experiences does matter to their educational opportunities and success.

In general, Black educators judge Black students' behavior more favorably than white educators (Rudd, 2014). Based on North Carolina student level data, Lindsay and Hart (2017) found that increased exposure to same-race educators reduced the rate of exclusionary discipline for Black students, and this finding was consistent across elementary, middle, and high school levels. Moreover, continued exposure to same-race teachers lowered Black students' discipline referrals for willful defiance. This study suggests that educators of color subconsciously value the humanity of students of color more so than white educators, and so hiring and increasing the representation of educators of color deeply matters to the care, educational success, and livelihood of children of color.

Address Not Just Implicit Racial Bias But Also Anti-Blackness

In our experience as professors who prepare K-12 teachers and educational leaders, we have yet to encounter an educator who is entering the profession for the wrong reasons, as they all profoundly care about making a difference in young people's lives. Nevertheless, even if an educator cares about their students, this level of care does not absolve them from playing out any unconscious racial biases they have towards students of color. We are all socialized by societal racial stereotypes that portray young Black people as more defiant, deviant, unruly, irresponsible, dishonest, and even dangerous (Rudd, 2014). Black educators can even internalize racial stereotypes about their own race, and these internalized stereotypes can have a negative effect on their treatment of Black children. Yet, Black educators are more likely to see Black students as worthy of receiving the benefit of the doubt (see Rudd, 2014). However, it is white cultural norms that dominate U.S. schooling, and so under the rubric of whiteness white children are allowed to make mistakes, but Black children are not (see Quereshi & Okonofua, 2017; Rudd, 2014).

Since we are all socialized by societal racial stereotypes, we all to some degree have implicit racial biases that can negatively affect how we perceive and interact with young people of color. Implicit racial bias is the "mental process that causes us to have negative feelings and attitudes about people" based on their racial identity (Quereshi & Okonofua, 2017, p. 3) Relying on our subconscious racial biases takes little effort, and we rely on racial stereotypes to make judgments and decisions when we encounter a racial or ethnic group we are unfamiliar with (Quereshi & Okonofua, 2017).

Instead of simply delivering interventions and strategies that improve or repair students' behaviors, educators should also do the mental work to critically examine how their own racial biases and practices contribute to racial disparities in school discipline. Thus, any interventions and strategies that serve as an alternative to exclusionary discipline must prioritize that educators' work on their own racial biases and examine how their biases negatively affect students of color.

However, perhaps even implicit racial bias is too soft a reason to explain why students of color receive harsher disciplinary consequences than their white peers. The way in which Black students, in particular, are seen as less worthy of redemption for their actions than white students begs the question, "Do we as educators truly value Black students' lives?". Ongoing professional development for and evaluation of teachers and principals should extend beyond just implicit racial bias but also include frank discussions about the prevalence of anti-Blackness in schools. It is only when we as educators are truthful about and acknowledge the institutional harm we place on Black and Brown students that we can then work to repair and undo this harm. Interventions and strategies that fail to critically examine educators' implicit racial biases and anti-Blackness that is pervasive in the school community do little to redress but instead reproduce racism in school discipline practices.

DISCUSSION QUESTIONS

1. What are your state level policies and/or stances on exclusionary discipline? How has your school district responded to and interpreted the state policy discourse on exclusionary discipline?
2. As the leader of your school, how do you communicate your expectations around student discipline? How does your racial identity contribute to your understanding of disciplinary practices? How might your expectations around discipline be racist?
3. Do you know the statistics on school discipline in your school district and across your state? How do these statistics differ for white and nonwhite students?
4. What alternatives do you have in place of disciplinary actions like school suspension? Do these alternatives directly address racism in discipline and require educators to examine their own implicit racial biases and anti-Blackness?
5. What can you do to make students, especially students of color, feel more included and connected to their school community?

SCHOOL DISCIPLINE RESOURCES

- African-American Policy Forum: https://aapf.org
- The Civil Rights Project/Proyecto Derechos Civiles: https://civilrightsproject.ucla.edu/research/k-12-education/school-discipline
- The Council of State Governments (CSG) Justice Policy Center: https://csgjusticecenter.org/
- Justice Policy Institute: www.justicepolicy.org/index.html
- NAACP Legal Defense and Education Fund: www.naacpldf.org

RECOMMENDED READINGS

Alexander, M. (2010). *The new Jim Crow: Mass incarceration in the era of colorblindness.* New York: The New Press.

Losen, D. J., Keith, II, M. A., Hodson, C. L., & Martinez, T. E. (2016). *Charter schools, civil rights and school discipline: A comprehensive review.* Los Angeles, CA: The Center for Civil Rights Remedies at The Civil Rights Project/Proyecto Derechos Civiles.

Milner, IV, H. R., Cunningham, H. B., Delale-O'Connor, L., & Kestenberg, E. G. (2019). *"These kids are out of control": Why we must reimagine "classroom management" for equity.* Thousand Oaks, CA: Corwin.

Okilwa, N. S., Khalifa, M., & Briscoe, F. (Eds.) (2017). *The school to prison pipeline: The role of culture & discipline in school.* Bingley, United Kingdom: Emerald Publishing Ltd.

Rumberger, R. W., & Losen, D. J. (2016). *The high cost of harsh discipline and its disparate impact.* Los Angeles, CA: The Center for Civil Rights Remedies at The Civil Rights Project/Proyecto Derechos Civiles.

Winn, M. T. (2018). *Justice on both sides: Transforming education through restorative justice.* Cambridge, MA: Harvard Education Press.

REFERENCES

The Advancement Project. (2014). *Restorative practices: Fostering healthy relationships & promoting positive discipline in schools: A guide for educators.* Cambridge, MA: The Schott Foundation for Public Education.

Ahmed, S., & Walker, C. (2018, May 25). There has been, on average, 1 school shooting every week this year. *CNN.* Retrieved from www.cnn.com/2018/03/02/us/school-shootings-2018-list-trnd/index.html

Alexander, M. (2010). *The new Jim Crow: Mass incarceration in the era of colorblindness.* New York: The New Press.

Anderson, K. P., & Ritter, G. W. (2017). Disparate use of exclusionary discipline evidence: Evidence on inequities in school discipline from a U.S. state. *Education Policy Analysis Archives, 25*(49). http://dx.doi.org/10.14507/epaa.25.2787

Barnum, M. (2016, March 27). Exclusive: Data shows 3 of the 5 biggest school districts hire more security officers than counselors. *The 74.* Retrieved from www.the74million.org/article/exclusive-data-shows-3-of-the-5-biggest-school-districts-hire-more-security-officers-than-counselors/

Barnum, M. (2019, February 14). New studies point to a big downside for schools bringing in more police. *Chalkbeat.* Retrieved from www.chalkbeat.org/posts/us/2019/02/14/police-schools-research-parkland/

Bonilla-Silva, E. (2017). *Racism without racists: Color-blind racism and the persistence of racial inequality in America* (5th edition). Lanham, MD: Rowman & Littlefield.

Committee for Children. (n.d.). *What is social-emotional learning?* Seattle, WA: Author. Retrieved from www.cfchildren.org/what-is-social-emotional-learning/

Corley, C. (2018). Do police officers in schools really make them safer. *NPR All Things Considered*. Retrieved from www.npr.org/2018/03/08/591753884/do-police-officers-in-schools-really-make-them-safer

The Council of State Governments Justice Center. (2017). *Realizing the full vision of school discipline reform: A framework for statewide change*. New York: Author.

DiAngelo, R. (2018). *White fragility: Why it's so hard for white people to talk about racism*. Boston, MA: Beacon Press.

Duncan, A. (2014). *Rethinking school discipline: Remarks of U.S. Secretary of Education Arne Duncan at the release of the joint DOJ-ED school discipline guidance package*. The Academies at Frederick Douglass High School, Baltimore, MD. Retrieved from www.ed.gov/news/speeches/rethinking-school-discipline

Fabelo, T., Thompson, M. D., Plotkin, M., Carmichael, D., Marchbanks, M. P., & Booth, E. A. (2011). *Breaking schools' rules: A statewide study of how school discipline relates to student's success and juvenile justice involvement*. New York: Council of State Governments Justice Center, and College Station, TX: Texas A&M University, Public Policy Research Institute.

Fausset, R., Pérez-Peña, R., & Blinder, A. (2015, October 28). Race and discipline in spotlight after South Carolina officer drags student. *The New York Times*. Retrieved from www.nytimes.com/2015/10/28/us/spring-valley-high-school-sc-officer-arrest.html

Finn, J. D., & Servoss, T. J. (2014). Misbehavior, suspensions, and security measures in high school: Racial/ethnic and gender differences. *Journal of Applied Research on Children: Informing Policy for Children at Risk, 5*(2), Article 11.

Fuchs, D., Mock, D., Morgan, P. L., & Young, C. L. (2003). Responsiveness to intervention: Definitions, evidence, and implications for the learning disabilities construct. *Learning Disabilities Research & Practice, 18*, 157–171.

Gershenson, S., Holt, S. B., & Papageorge, N. (2016). Who believes in me? The effect of student-teacher demographic match on teacher expectations. *Economics of Education Review, 52*, 209–224.

Gilliam, W. S., Maupin, A. N., Reyes, C. R., Accavitti, M., & Shic, F. (2016). *Do early educators' implicit biases regarding sex and race relate to behavior expectations and recommendations of expulsions and suspensions?* New Haven, CT: Yale University Child Care Center.

Gopalan, M., & Nelson. A. A. (2019). Understanding the racial discipline gap in schools. *AERA Open*. https://doi.org/10.1177/2332858419844613

The Journal of Blacks in Higher Education. (2019). *Racial disparities in school discipline have little to do with student behavior*. Retrieved from www.jbhe.com/2019/07/racial-disparities-in-school-discipline-have-little-to-do-with-different-student-behavior/

Keierleber, M. (2019). Lessons from Parkland: 6 big things we've learned about student safety, school security, and resilience since the tragic 2018 massacre.

The 74. Retrieved from www.the74million.org/lessons-from-parkland-6-big-things-weve-learned-about-student-safety-school-security-and-resilience-since-the-tragic-2018-massacre/

Lewis, C., Butler, B., Bonner, F., & Joubert, M. (2010). African American male discipline patterns and school district responses resulting impact on academic achievement: Implications for urban educators and policy makers. *Journal of African American Males in Education, 1*(1), 8–25.

Lindsay, C. A., & Hart, C. M. D. (2017). Exposure to same-race teachers and student disciplinary outcomes for Black students in North Carolina. *Educational Evaluation and Policy Analysis, 39*(3), 485–510.

Lindsay, C. A., Lee, V., & Lloyd, T. (2018). *The prevalence of police officers in U.S. Schools.* Urban Institute. Retrieved from www.urban.org/urban-wire/prevalence-police-officers-us-schools

Mansfield, K. C., Rainbolt, S., & Fowler., E. S. (2018). Implementing restorative justice as a step toward racial equity in school discipline. *Teachers College Record, 120*(14), 1–24.

Mattison, E., & Aber, M. S. (2007). Closing the achievement gap: The association of racial climate with achievement and behavioral outcomes. *American Journal of Community Psychology, 40*(1), 1–12.

McNeely, C. A., Nonemaker, J. M., & Blum, R. W. (2002). Promoting student connectedness to school: From the national longitudinal study of adolescent health. *Journal of School Health, 72*(4), 138–147.

Milner, IV, H. R., Cunningham, H. B., Delale-O'Connor, L., & Kestenberg, E.G. (2019). *"These Kids are out of control": Why we must reimagine "classroom management "for equity.* Thousand Oaks, CA: Corwin.

Na, C., & Gottfredson, D. C. (2013). Police officers in schools: Effects on school crime and the processing of offending behaviors. *Justice Quarterly, 30*(4), 619–650.

National Child Traumatic Stress Network Schools Committee (NCTSN). (2017). *Creating, supporting, and sustaining trauma-informed schools: A system framework.* Los Angeles, CA, and Durham, NC: National Center for Child Traumatic Stress.

National Clearinghouse on Supportive School Discipline (NCSSD). (n.d.). *Pushout.* Retrieved from https://supportiveschooldiscipline.org/learn/reference-guides/pushout

Owens, J., & McLanahan, S. S. (2019). Unpacking the drivers of racial disparities in school suspension and expulsion. *Social Forces*, 1–30. DOI: 10.1093/sf/soz095.

Petteruti, A. (2011). *Education under arrest: The case against policy in schools.* Washington, D.C.: Justice Policy Institute. Retrieved from www.justicepolicy.org/uploads/justicepolicy/documents/educationunderarrest_fullreport.pdf

Quereshi, A., & Okonofua, J. (2017). *Locked out of the classroom: How implicit bias contributes to disparities in school discipline.* New York: NAACP Legal Defense Fund. Retrieved from www.naacpldf.org/files/about-us/Bias_Reportv2017_30_11_FINAL.pdf

Rafa, A. (2018). *Alternative school discipline strategies.* Denver, CO: Education Commission of the States. Retrieved from www.ecs.org/alternative-school-discipline-strategies/

Rafa, A. (2019). *The status of school discipline in state policy.* Denver, CO: Education Commission of the States. Retrieved from www.ecs.org/the-status-of-school-discipline-in-state-policy/

Rausch, K. M., & Skiba, R. J. (2006). *The academic cost of discipline: The contribution of school discipline to achievement.* Bloomington, IN: Indiana University, Center for Evaluation and Education Policy.

RTI Action Network. (n.d.). *What is RTI?* Retrieved from www.rtinetwork.org/learn/what/whatisrti

Rudd, T. (2014, February). *Racial disproportionality in school discipline: Implicit bias is heavily implicated.* Columbus, OH: Kirwan Institute, The Ohio State University. Retrieved from http://kirwaninstitute.osu.edu/racial-disproportionality-in-school-discipline-implicit-bias-is-heavily-implicated/

Sanchez, J. I. (2015). VOYCE's groundbreaking bill, SB 100, to address "school-to-prison pipeline" passes Illinois legislature. Retrieved from http://voyceproject.org/2015/05/21/groundbreaking-bill-sb-100-to-address-school-to-prison-pipeline-passes-illinois-legislature/

Skiba, R. J. (2015). Interventions to address racial/ethnic disparities in school discipline: Can systems reform be race-neutral? In R. Bangs, & L. E. Davis (Eds.), *Race and social problems: Restructuring inequality* (pp. 107–124). New York: Springer Science + Business Media.

Skiba, R. J., Arredondo, M. I., & Williams, N. T. (2017). In and of itself a risk factor: Exclusionary discipline and the school-to-prison pipeline. In K. J. Fasching-Varner, L. L. Martin, R. W. Mitchell, K. P. Bennett-Haron, & A. Daneshzadeh. (Eds). *Understanding dismantling, and disrupting the prison-to-school pipeline* (pp. 111–130). Lanham, MD: Rowman & Littlefield.

Steinberg, M. P., & Lacoe, J. (2017). What do we know about school discipline reform? *Education Next, 17*(1), 1–23.

Theriot, M. T. (2009). School resource officers and the criminalization of student behavior. *Journal of Criminal Justice, 37*(3), 280–287.

United States Commission on Civil Rights. (2019). *Beyond suspensions: Examining school discipline policies and connections to the school-to-prison pipeline for students of color with disabilities.* Washington, D.C.: Author. Retrieved from www.usccr.gov/pubs/2019/07-23-Beyond-Suspensions.pdf

United States Department of Education Office for Civil Rights. (2014). *Civil rights data collection data snapshot: Early childhood data collection.* Issue Brief No. 2. Retrieved from https://ocrdata.ed.gov/Downloads/CRDC-Early-Childhood-Education-Snapshot.pdf

United States Department of Education Office for Civil Rights. (n.d.). *2015–2016 civil rights data collection: Master list of 2015–2016 CRDC definitions.* Retrieved from https://ocrdata.ed.gov/Downloads/Master-List-of-CRDC-Definitions.pdf

United States Department of Education Office for Civil Rights. (2018). *2015–2016 Civil rights data collection: School climate and safety.* Retrieved from https://www2.ed.gov/about/offices/list/ocr/docs/school-climate-and-safety.pdf

United States Government Accountability Office. (2018). *K-12 education discipline disparities for Black students, boys, and students with disabilities.* Retrieved from www.gao.gov/assets/700/690828.pdf

Vanderhaar, J. E., Petrosko, J. M., & Munoz, M. (2015). Reconsidering the alternatives: The relationship between suspension, disciplinary alternative school placement, subsequent juvenile detention, and the salience of race. In D. J. Losen (Ed.), *Closing the school discipline gap: Research for policymakers* (pp. 222–236). New York: Teachers College Press.

Vidal, G. (2019, November 1). Manor ISD moves forward with plans for its own police department. *CBS Austin.* Retrieved from https://cbsaustin.com/news/local/manor-isd-moves-forward-with-plans-for-its-own-police-department

Welsh, R. O., & Little, S. (2018). The school discipline dilemma: A comprehensive review of disparities and alternative approaches. *Review of Educational Research, 88*(5), 752–794.

Welton, A. D., Harris, T. O., Altamirano, K., & Williams, T. (2017). The politics of student voice. Conceptualizing a model for critical analysis. In M. D. Young & S. Diem (Eds.), *Critical approaches to education policy analysis. Moving beyond tradition* (pp. 83–110). Switzerland: Springer International Publishing.

Welton, A., & Bertrand, M. (2019). Youth participatory action research as praxis: The importance of shared power among youth and adults to counter systemic racism. In A. Dache, S. J. Quaye, C. Linder, & K. M. McGuire (Eds.), *Rise Up!: Activism as Education* (pp. 49–68). East Lansing, MI: Michigan State University Press.

Chapter 8

A Protocol for Anti-Racist Policy Decision-Making in Educational Leadership

Each color-evasive and market-driven policy problem we presented in Chapters 2 through 7 is indeed systemic in nature. Hence, the solutions designed to remedy the racial wrongs that are a consequence of these policies can by no means be piecemeal, simplistic, band-aid approaches that address only one element of policy problems that are quite complex. Because the racism that results from these neoliberal policies manifests systemically, leaders then need to combat these same policy problems in a systemic manner. So, in order to confront neoliberal, racist policies systemically educational leaders need to be willing to dismantle the racist ideologies, structures, and processes linked to these policies. Although shifting to a race-conscious ideological outlook at the individual level is important, anti-racism also requires a commitment to action-orientated change at the systemic level (Dei, 1996; Welton, Owens, & Zamani-Gallaher, 2018). Thus, we envision anti-racist educational leadership as the best approach to combatting neoliberal, racist policies systemically.

In this chapter we introduce an anti-racist policy decision-making protocol to help educational leaders confront color-evasive and market-driven educational policies systemically. We liken our protocol to an equity audit, where educators systematically engage in a cycle of inquiry to unmask inequities deeply entrenched within the district and/or school norms, policies, structures, and practices (Capper & Young, 2015; Frattura & Capper, 2007; View et al., 2016). Typically, educational leaders use equity audits to systematically collect and examine data to identify equity gaps, and this process is accomplished in a series of phases (Capper & Young, 2015). For example, Capper and Young's (2015) framework for an equity audit includes the following six phases: (1) identify integrated/inclusive practices as measured by proportional representation as the foundational philosophy of the equity audit, (2) establish the team to conduct the audit, (3) design the audit, (4) collect and analyze the data, (5) set and prioritize goals based on the data, and (6) develop an implementation plan to reach the goals that includes review of the goals and plan (p. 190). Similarly, Green (2017) extended beyond just the school as the unit of analysis for an equity audit and developed a community-based equity audit for educational leaders that includes the following four phases: (1) disrupt deficit views of the community, (2) conduct initial community inquiry and shared community experiences, (3) establish a Community Leadership Team (CLT), and (4) collect equity, asset-based community data for action (p. 17).

In addition to equity audit frameworks, a few equity-centered policy analysis models informed the development of our anti-racist policy decision-making protocol for educational leaders. For example, a series of policy analysis tools designed on behalf of the Great Lakes Equity Assistance Center consider how a diverse set of stakeholders can come together to critique systemic policies significant to the school community (Kyser, Skelton, Warren, & Whiteman, 2016; Macey, Thorius, & Skelton, 2012). Kyser et al. (2016) suggest that when school and community stakeholders come together to engage in a policy analysis process that it be rooted in critical reflection that reveals the intended and unintended consequences of the policy. Therefore, critical reflection on policy

> requires us to examine both written and unwritten policies. We must question our intentions, assumptions, and the distribution of resources and opportunities.
>
> (Kyser et al., 2016, p. 6)

Similarly, Rallis et al. (2008) designed a policy analysis framework that drives educational leaders to consider whether the policy under consideration and its subsequent implementation are just and ethical. Adopting a similar premise to these equity-centered policy analysis models, our policy decision-making protocol exposes the systemic racism that is a result of market-driven policies per the following six phases (see Figure 8.1): (1) assemble the appropriate team, (2) set expectations for the team, (3) understand the sociopolitical and racial

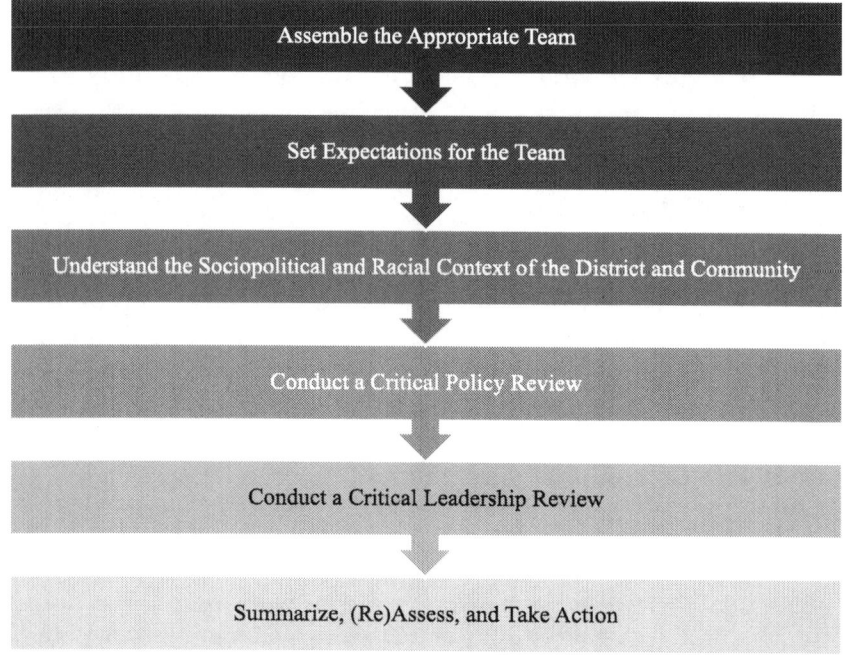

Figure 8.1 Anti-racist policy decision-making protocol for educational leaders

context of the district and community, (4) conduct a critical policy review, (5) conduct a critical leadership review, and (6) summarize, (re)assess, and take action. Subsequently, in this chapter we outline in detail the six phases of our anti-racist policy decision-making protocol for educational leaders.

ANTI-RACIST POLICY DECISION-MAKING PROTOCOL FOR EDUCATIONAL LEADERS

Step 1 – Assemble the Appropriate Team

School leaders alone cannot address racial inequities in their school communities. They need colleagues who can also take leadership roles throughout their schools to ensure policies are implemented with an anti-racist mindset and understanding of the neoliberal context in which education operates, which in turn can lead to more just and equitable school environments (see Green, 2017). So, prior to deciding how a policy will be implemented and the racial implications for said policy, school leaders need to assemble an appropriate team who can best address the policy issue. We recommend school leaders consider a number of questions when putting together a team.

Guiding Questions

1. What is the constitution of the team? Have you weighed the pros and cons of a small vs. large team?
2. Have you ensured the team has diverse representation (e.g., in terms of diversity and expertise)?
3. Are there enough team members with knowledge about the policy issue? If not, how will you make sure to include such experts/key stakeholders?
4. Are there enough team members with experience engaging in race-related work? If not, how will you work with the community to include such experts/key stakeholders?
5. What will each team member be responsible for and how will decisions about such duties be made, and by whom?

Key Recommendations

- It is critical to consider what key stakeholders—internal and external to the school setting—are integral to the policy analysis process and how they can be included in the conversation. It is important to take the time to determine who these individuals are and what their potential roles can be as members of the team.
- Similarly, it is important to include members of the team with experience centering anti-racist practices in their work. If such individuals do not exist in the school district, it is imperative to reach out to professionals working in the community who can contribute to this important piece of the team. Consider non-profit organizations or other community-based organizations (CBOs) whose mission specifically addresses racial justice and bring them to the table.
- Ensuring diverse representation is present should be intentional and reflect the demographics of the school community. Diverse perspectives are critical to bring to the conversation and help to provide a more nuanced and holistic understanding of policies and their racial implications for schools.

Step 2 – Set Expectations for the Team

Once the team is assembled, it is important to establish clear expectations for the work of the team. Collectively, the team should come to an agreement around the goals and expectations associated with the work of the team. The team should also establish clear rules and norms when meeting in person and when working together outside of meeting times. Conversations around race can be very contentious and people can become very passionate when it comes to the insidious impacts of every day racism. We want people to be passionate about eradicating racism in their schools and communities but we also have to remember people are entering the conversation with diverse experiences and perspectives. We therefore suggest a number of factors to consider as you begin the process of setting team expectations.

Guiding Questions
1. What is the reason for conducting a policy analysis?
2. What is the goal of the process?
3. Has the team collectively agreed on rules and norms?
4. If one or two people do not agree with the rules and norms, how will you as the leader of the team listen to their concerns, make sure they feel listened to despite not being part of the majority, and make sure a compromise is reached among the team members?
5. How will you navigate potentially needing to change team expectations as the work progresses and ideas or goals shift?
6. How will you make sure team meetings provide a space where everyone feels valued and part of the conversation?
7. How will you make sure team meetings provide a space for consistent personal and group reflection on the work of the team, particularly when it comes to race?

Key Recommendations
- Ask every team member to write a racial autobiography prior to the first team meeting and share these with the group. Racial autobiographies can assist in team members developing a greater racial awareness, gain more insight into their colleagues' racial experiences, and cultivate anti-racist mindsets that may then lead to anti-racist practices (Gooden & O'Doherty, 2015).
- Use Leonardo and Porter's (2010) article, "Pedagogy of fear: Toward a Fanonian theory of 'safety' in race dialogue," which

addresses "the myth of safety in race dialogue for people of color" as a starting point on how to engage in cross-racial dialogues as a team *and* better comprehend why people of color may not necessarily feel "safe" in public race discussions. Often facilitators of racial dialogues work to establish a "safe" space for participants to engage in these discussions, but according to Leonardo and Porter creating "safety" or "safe spaces" is a "misnomer" that in reality is designed to make white people feel safe and comfortable in these discussions. However, creating this safety ultimately is "oppressive" to people of color as well as color-evasive because it protects white people from participating in racial dialogue so that they don't have to "feel racist" (p. 147).
- Engage in consistent reflections about race with the team, particularly in terms of how the policy under analysis may contribute to racial inequities.
- Welcome discomfort, suspend judgement, stay engaged, and expect challenges throughout the process (Kyser et al., 2016).

Step 3 – Understand the Sociopolitical and Racial Context of the District and Community

Context matters and is critical to understanding how policy and practice are shaped and implemented. Understanding the racial context of the district and community, including how it may have changed over time, the students being served, and how the sociopolitical context has played a role in addressing the needs of the district and community, both historically and contemporarily, can help to frame a well-informed and comprehensive policy agenda (Green, 2017). Politics and those with key political roles can affect the durability of policies, how and who is making decisions around the policies, and why such decisions are made (Diem, 2012). We therefore suggest considering a number of different items related to the sociopolitical and racial contexts of your district and community as you engage in your policy analysis processes.

Guiding Questions
1. What is the demographic make-up of your school and community?
2. How has the demographic make-up of your school and community changed over time?
3. What is the political context of your school and community?

4. What are the policy interests of your school board?
5. How has racial equity and anti-racism been addressed in school and district policy?
6. What are the policy interests of your city council and mayor? What does the education policy agenda include for the city? How is racial equity and anti-racism addressed in the city in regards to education and schooling?

Key Recommendations
- Identify school districts and communities that have engaged in racial equity work specific to the policy you are currently examining. Determine the successes and challenges they experienced during the process as well as lessons learned.
- Assemble historical documents from your school, district, and local community to better understand how policy has changed over time, who the key players have been in the process, and what positions have been taken for or against a policy issue.
- Collect demographic data on your school district and community from such databases as the U.S. Census, state departments of education, and the National Center for Education Statistics.
- Identify where racial equity work is occurring in your community.
- Research education policy agendas for your local representatives, city council members, and mayor.

Step 4 – Conduct a Critical Policy Review

With each policy problem we reviewed in this book we demonstrate what happens when policy makers and school leaders fail to consider the racial consequences of the policies they either develop or are faced with implementing. A major problem with the neoliberal educational policies that now dominate public policy is that these policies have economic and individual goals instead of a humanistic aim that serves the public good (Horsford, Scott, & Anderson, 2019). To confront neoliberal agendas, district/school level policy actors must instead try to humanize the policy under review by bearing in mind how certain groups would be differentially affected upon the policy's implementation. Thus, we use research on critical approaches to policy analysis to inform Step 4, conducting a critical policy review (see Horsford et al., 2019). At a fundamental level, a critical policy review involves questioning the nature of the policy, how it evolved, and any assumptions about the extent of the policy's impact (Young & Diem, 2017). Yet from an anti-racist perspective, a critical policy review also questions any policy rhetoric, uncovers racial hierarchies entrenched in the political process, interrogates if and how the policy inequitably distributes power and resources along racial lines, and ensures the perspectives of racially minoritized groups are centered in the policy process (also see Horsford et al., 2019). Therefore, drawing from critical policy analysis approaches we provide suggestions for guiding questions and recommendations for conducting a critical policy review.

Guiding Questions
1. What are the intentions of the policy and what does it aim to accomplish?
2. How do the policy intentions align with what happens on the ground in day-to-day practice? Are the policy intentions realistic?
3. Who benefits from the policy and who is negatively affected? Consider how this policy will affect racially minoritized groups.
4. Who has a voice in the policy process and whose voice is currently silenced? Are the voices of racially minoritized groups elevated in the policy process?
5. Overall, is the policy racially just? Would implementing the policy result in ethically questionable practices? (Kyser et al. 2016; Rallis et al., 2008)

Key Recommendations
- First, ensure team members are educated on how the policy process works. The policy process is a series of events that unfold when a political system deliberates on different approaches to a policy problem, adopts a policy approach, and then implements and evaluates the chosen policy (Fowler, 2012).
- Before reviewing the policy, the team should understand how policies become racialized in the U.S. context. Have the team engage in key readings that reflect on race, racism, and public policy; and devote time to discussing as a team how the policy problems presented in the readings compare to the policy issue under review. Some suggestions to start with would be *Racial Formation in the United States, 3rd edition* by Michael Omi and Howard Winant; *White Rage: The Unspoken Truth of Our Racial*

Divide by Carol Anderson; and *The Color of Law: A Forgotten History of How our Government Segregated America* by Richard Rothstein.
- Conduct both an individual and team review of the policy. Use the guiding questions for Step 4 to assist with the policy review.
- Consider what additional information you may need to answer the guiding questions for this step. Do you need to gather feedback from additional district/school stakeholders via focus groups or forums, or perhaps surveys? Perhaps you need to do research to see how the policy was implemented in other contexts and existing data on the policy outcomes as well.

Step 5 – Conduct a Critical Leadership Review

Both district and school level leaders not only have to interpret policies that come from above (federal and state level) but develop and implement policies as well (Rallis et al., 2008). No matter where the policy derives from, educational leaders are still charged with communicating the policy to the school community. However, what is most ideal is for educational leaders to interpret policies *with* the school community. At this stage educational leaders should take a step back and critically examine the extent to which they are engaging in democratic deliberation where various viewpoints are considered in the dialogue about the policy (Rallis et al., 2008). The guiding questions and key recommendations we present below push educational leaders to consider how at this stage of the policy process they are engaging in what Horsford, Scott, and Anderson (2109) coin as *democracy-driven decision-making* where educational leaders recognize that the critical review of the policy should be "community-centric" where there is shared-power with the school community in the decision-making process (p. 198).

Guiding Questions
1. To what extent are you promoting shared leadership on the decision-making team? Is there shared power and do opportunities exist for those who do not hold formal school leadership roles such as parents, students, and community members from racially minoritized groups to co-lead?
2. How authentic is the participation in dialogue on the decision-making team, and is it rooted in anti-racism? (see Anderson, 1998)
3. How is the information discussed on the team communicated to the rest of the school community, particularly members of racially minoritized groups?

Key Recommendations

- While we recommend considering distributed forms of leadership that are rooted in equity and social justice (Brooks, Jean-Marie, Normore, & Hodgins, 2007), leaders should go a step further and critique the level of authenticity of participation and shared leadership (Anderson, 1998; also see Horsford et al., 2019). Anderson's (1998) framework for authentic participation posits five questions for leaders when considering the level of authenticity of participation at the micro and macro levels:

    (a) Participation toward what end? (b) Who participates? (c) What are relevant spheres of participation? (d) What conditions and processes must be present locally to make participation authentic (i.e., the micropolitics of participation)? (e) What conditions and processes must be present at broader institutional and societal levels (i.e., the macropolitics of participation).

    (p. 587)

- We also recommend that leaders look to research on grassroots community organizing for specific strategies on shared leadership. The principal, superintendent, and other formal administrators are the archetypes that first come to mind for educational leadership, but successful leadership takes more than a single person, and so community organizing is a school improvement strategy that relies on shared leadership *with* the community and can serve as a conduit for "breaking down power relationships between parents, teachers, and school officials" (Carlock, 2016, p. 118; Welton & Freelon, 2018).

Step 6 – Summarize, (Re)assess, and Take Action

In this final step, the decision-making team should summarize findings from the previous five steps and develop a plan of how to communicate the findings to the rest of the school community. Next, the team should come up with a few possible courses of action and get feedback from the school community on which action plan best aligns with anti-racist change that centers the needs and perspectives of racially minoritized groups. Once the plan of action is selected, team members should delineate the timeline of implementation and how members of the team will be accountable for carrying out various aspects of the plan. Finally, once the action plan has been carried out, time should be dedicated to reassessing the plan of action, what did and did not work, and what changes need to occur before engaging in the process again for the next policy issue on the docket. Hence, we envision these six steps as a cycle of inquiry that can be repeated.

Guiding Questions
1. What policy actions will you take given your understanding of the policy and what will you prioritize in your action planning?
2. Consider the policy problem systemically. What mindset shifts, changes in norms, structures, and even redistribution of resources would lead to the type of anti-racist change needed to address the policy problem?
3. Given what you know about the policy and from your understanding of leadership, what types of leadership moves and practices would you use to respond to the policy problem and take action?
4. What types of risks are you willing to take when taking action? How will you respond to pushback and resistance from some members of the school community based on the team's decision?
5. What resources and supports will you need to carry out the action plan?
6. How will you hold team members accountable for carrying out the action plan, and what is your plan for assessing progress moving forward?

Key Recommendations
- In this final step before taking action, the decision-making team should weigh in on various courses of action they could take and assess the type of risk involved with each option, as well as what level of risk they are willing to take to achieve real anti-racist change.
- To prepare for potential stakeholder pushback and resistance when the plan of action for anti-racist change is carried out, we suggest team members refer to research on educator activism (Marshall & Anderson, 2008) and racial justice activists (Gorski & Erakat, 2019). An activist is "an individual who is known for taking stands and engaging in action aimed at producing social change, possibly in conflict with institutional opponents" (Marshall & Anderson, 2008, p. 18). When racial justice activists upend the

racial status quo in their school communities they are taking a great risk to do so—a risk that could jeopardize their job security and sever friendships and relational ties, which could all then lead to burnout and fatigue (Marshall & Anderson, 2008; Gorski & Erakat, 2019). Consequently, members of the decision-making team need to prepare themselves for the political and emotional labor that comes with anti-racist change and activism.

CONCLUDING THOUGHTS

What we are proposing in this anti-racist policy decision-making protocol is just one of the many responses to a color-evasive, market-driven educational policy context. However, to truly achieve racial equality in education, other social institutions outside of education must also radically restructure and work toward operating with a truly democratic mindset. Education has always been thought of as the answer to all of society's ills because it is one of the only socialized institutions still in existence. Yet our education system cannot counteract rising income inequality or residential segregation in a political context that has retreated from desegregation or health care access and affordability—all of which are deeply intertwined with race *and* have a direct impact on education. A just and anti-racist society cannot exist without an awareness of racism *and* a commitment to and investment in anti-racism by institutions and individuals alike. It is our hope that our book will help educational leaders acknowledge how they may contribute to the racial inequities that are a consequence of neoliberal ideologies in the larger societal context and then act to dismantle them in their school communities and beyond.

REFERENCES

Anderson, C. (2016). *White rage: The unspoken truth of our racial divide.* New York: Bloomsbury.

Anderson, G. L. (1998). Toward authentic participation: Deconstructing the discourses of participatory reforms in education. *American Educational Research Journal, 35*(4), 571–603.

Brooks, J., Jean-Marie, G., Normore, A., & Hodgins, D. (2007). Distributed leadership for social justice: Exploring how influence and equity are stretched over an urban high school. *Journal of School Leadership, 17*(4), 378–408.

Capper, C., & Young, M. D. (2015). The equity audit as the core of leading increasing diverse schools and districts. In G. Theoharis & M. Scanlan (Eds.), *Leadership for increasingly diverse schools* (pp. 186–197). New York: Routledge.

Carlock, Jr., R. H. (2016). La union hace la fuerza: Community organizing in adult education for immigrants. *Harvard Educational Review, 86*(1), 98–122.

Dei, G. J. S. (1996). Critical perspectives in antiracism: An introduction. *Canadian Review of Sociology, 33*(3), 247–267.

Diem, S. (2012). The relationship between policy design, context, and implementation in integration plans. *Education Policy Analysis Archives, 20*(23), 1–39.

Fowler, F. (2012). *Policy studies for educational leaders: An introduction.* Upper Saddle Ridge, NJ: Pearson-Merrill Prentice Hall.

Frattura, E. M., & Capper, C. A. (2007). *Leading for social justice: Transforming schools for all leaders.* Thousand Oaks, CA: Corwin Press.

Gooden, M. A., & O'Doherty, A. (2015). Do you see what I see? Fostering aspiring leaders' racial awareness. *Urban Education, 50*(2), 225–255.

Gorski, P. C., & Erakat, N. (2019). Racism, whiteness, and burnout in antiracism movements: How white racial activists elevate burnout in racial justice activist of color in the United States. *Ethnicities.* DOI: 10.1177/1468796819833871

Green, T. L. (2017). Community-based equity audits: A practical approach for educational leaders to support equitable community-school improvements. *Educational Administration Quarterly, 53*(1), 3–39.

Horsford, S. D., Scott, J. T., & Anderson, G. L. (2019). *The politics of education policy in an era of inequality: Possibilities for democratic schooling.* New York: Routledge.

Kyser, T. S., Skelton, S. M., Warren, C. L., & Whiteman, R. S. (2016). *Policy equity analysis toolkit.* Indianapolis, IN: Great Lakes Equity Center. Retrieved from http://glec.education.iupui.edu/Images/equity_tools/2016_03_25_Policy%20Toolkit_FINAL.pdf

Leonardo, Z., & Porter, R. K. (2010). Pedagogy of fear: Toward a Fanonian theory of "safety" in race dialogue. *Race Ethnicity and Education, 13*(2), 139–157.

Macey, E. M., Thorius, K. A. K., & Skelton, S. M. (2012). *Equity by design: Engaging school communities in critical reflection on policy.* Indianapolis, IN: Great Lakes Equity Center. Retrieved from http://glec.education.iupui.edu/assets/files/2013_5_1_PolicyBrief_FINAL.pdf

Marshall, C., & Anderson, A. L. (Eds.). (2008). *Activist educators: Breaking past limits.* New York: Routledge.

Omi, M., & Winant, H. (2015). *Racial formation in the United States, 3rd edition.* New York: Routledge.

Rallis, S., Rossman, G., Reagan, T., Cobb, C., & Kuntz, A. (2008). *Leading dynamic schools: How to create and implement ethical policies.* Thousand Oaks, CA: Corwin Press.

Rothstein, R. (2017). *The color of law: A forgotten history of how our government segregated America*. New York: Liveright Publishing Corporation.

View, J. L., DeMulder, E., Stribling, S., Dodman, S., Ra, S., Hall, B., & Swalwell, K. (2016). Equity audit: A teacher leadership tool for nurturing teacher research. *The Educational Forum, 80*(4), 380–393.

Welton, A. D., & Freelon, R. (2018). Community organizing as educational leadership: Lessons from Chicago on the politics of racial justice. *Journal of Research on Leadership Education, 13*(1), 79–104.

Welton, A. D., Owens, D. R., & Zamani-Gallaher, E. M. (2018). Anti-racist change: A conceptual framework for educational institutions to take systemic action. *Teachers College Record, 120*(14).

Young, M. D., & Diem, S. (Eds.). (2017). *Critical approaches to education policy analysis: Moving beyond tradition*. Switzerland: Springer International Publishing.

Index

Note: Page numbers in *italics* refer to figures; those in **bold** refer to tables.

Abbott v. Burke (1985) 104–105
Aber, M. S. 117
ableism 8–9
achievement gaps 29, 42, 82–83, 84, 85, 108; data and analysis 84
action-orientated change 138; decision-making protocol 147–149
activism, from communities of color 72–74
adequacy funding frameworks 101–109
Adequate Yearly Progress (AYP) 59
Alamo Heights Independent School District 103
Alexander, Michelle 115
American Federation of Teachers 42
Anderson, K. P. 120
Annamma, S. A. 8, 9
anti-Blackness 5–6, 131–132
anti-racism, definition 3
anti-racist leadership 2–4, 32; to combat racist policies 138–149; and data-driven decision-making (DDDM) 90–91; decision-making protocol 14, *140*, 142–149; and school choice 47–51; and school closure 72–74; and school funding 109–110; and strategies for discipline 128–132
anti-Semitism 26
Arkansas, disproportionate discipline in schools 120–121
Arredondo, M. I. 116
Asian students, stereotypes of 31
Au, W. 11
Austin, Texas 73
Austin Voices for Education and Youth (AVEY) 73

Baker, B. D. 107
Berkeley Unified School District (BUSD) 49
Berube, A. 23
Bilingual Multicultural Education Act (1978) 107
bipartisanship: responsibility for prison industrial complex 115; support for school choice policies 46; support for school closures 59; support sought by

President Obama 86, 87; of white supremacy 27
Black, capitalization of 17–18
Black educators, hiring as success measure 130
Black students: and Black educators 130, 131; disadvantaged by voucher programs 43–44; disproportionate discipline of 115–116, 117–118, 120–121, 124–125, 129; experience in white schools 40; impact of school closures 59–60, 64, 65, 70–72; and magnet schools 41; overall school experience 5–6; percentage of school enrollment 24, **25;** and policing in schools 123–124; segregation in schools 24–25
Black voters, share of vote 23
Black-white achievement gap 29, 42, 84, 85
Blackstone Valley Prep school, Rhode Island 49
Bloomberg, Michael (Mayor of NYC 2002–2013) 69
Brexit 26
Brown, Michael 120
Brown v. Board of Education (1954) 10, 30, 40, 43
Brown v. Board of Education II (1955) 40
Brummet, Q. 72
Buckley, J. 45
budgets *see* funding
Burkholder, Z. 4
Bush, George H. W. (President of the United States 1989–93) 82
Bush, George W. (President of the United States 2001–09) 28, 59, 82, 84–85

California educational policies 28–29, 101–102
Campaign for Fiscal Equity v. State of New York (2003) 106

Capitol Region Education Council (CREC) 50
Capper, C. 139
Carlson, D. 72
Center on Budget and Policy Priorities 98
Charlottesville white nationalist rally 2017 26
charter schools 42–43, 45, 61–63; diverse-by-design 49–50
Chicago, Illinois: federal involvement in education policies 81; policing in schools 122
Chicago Public Schools (CPS) closures: academic decline of students 71; adverse effect on parental involvement 67–68; community hunger strikes 73–74; disproportionate effect on Black students 69; explanations for 61, 64; mass closure 59–60; race and equitable access 65, *66;* reinforcing racial segregation 67; student enrollment decline 72
Chicago youth organizers 129
City Garden Montessori School, St. Louis 50
civil rights 1, 80, 84, 122, 124
Civil Rights Act (1964) 41, 80, 115
Civil Rights Movement 11, 82
Clinton, William Jefferson (Bill) (President of the United States 1993–2001) 27, 115
Cobb, C. 139
Collaborative for Equity and Justice in Education (University of Illinois) 67
color-evasiveness 6–9, 26, 30; and alternative discipline strategies 127–128; and the No Child Left Behind Act 82–85; origins of concept 7; and school choice 38, 45; and school closure 60–63, 70–72; and school discipline 120–121; and standardized testing 12, 82–85

colorblindness: challenging use of term 8–9; *see also* color-evasiveness
Columbine High School shooting 119, 122
communities: activism by 73–74; as stakeholders in assessment development 91
community nucleus, schools as 73
controlled-choice student assignment 48–49
crime incidence on routes to school 65–67
Cruz-Guzman v. Minnesota (2018) 29

Daley, Richard M. (Mayor of Chicago 1955–1976) 69
Dancy II, T. E. 6
Darling-Hammond, L. 97, 109
data-driven decision-making (DDDM): anti-racist 91; flaws under the No Child Left Behind Act 83–85
data use 16
Davis, J. E. 6
de la Torre, M. 61, 71
decision-making protocol 142–149
demographic change 15; diversity increase 23; gentrification 24; resistance and responses 30
Detroit: school closures 60, 62, 72; state takeover 62–63, 81
DeVos, Betsy (Secretary of Education 2017–) 44, 46
DiAngelo, R. 4, 5
Diliberti, M. 24
disabilities: dis/abilities, deficit model 8–9; disaggregation of data 120; funding for students with 83, 88, 98, 102; inequity of education for students with 107
discipline in schools 16–17; alternative strategies to exclusion 125–128; and race 120–121; racial injustice at preschool 115–116; *see also* Black students: disproportionate discipline of
diverse-by-design charter schools 49–50
Dumas, M. J. 5, 6
Duncan, Arne (Secretary of Education 2009–2015) 65, 69
Dyett High School, Chicago 74

EdBuild report (2019) 99
Edgewood Independent School District v. Kirby (1984) 103–104
education as a fundamental right: Kentucky 105–106; New Mexico 106–107; New York 106
Education Week 98
educational leadership *see* anti-racist leadership; leadership
Edwards, K. T. 6
Ee, J. 24
Elementary Secondary Education Act 1965 (ESEA) 16, 80–82
Emanuel, Rahm (Mayor of Chicago 2011–2019) 65
Engberg, J. 71
English Learners (EL) 28, 98, 102
Enjeti, A. 31
Equal Protection Clause (Amendment XIV 1868) 101, 103
equity audits 17, 138–139
equity evaluation of U.S. states 89
ERASE framework 91
ethnoburbs 31
Every Student Succeeds Act (ESSA) 2015 12, 16, 80; comparisons with No Child Left Behind Act 87–90
exclusionary discipline 118

Farrie, D. 107
Fenty, Adrian (District of Columbia Mayor 2007–2011) 69
Ferrare, J. J. 11
finance *see* funding

Finn, J. D. 124
Finnigan, K. S. 91
Fordham Institute 72
Forrest Cataldi, E. 24
Frankenberg, E. 24
Frankenberg, R. 7, 9
Friedman, Milton 40
funding 16; gap between white and nonwhite districts 99–100; landmark school finance cases 100–107; role of school leaders 109–110; statistical overview 97–100

Gaertner, M. 70
gang activity and routes to school 65–67
gentrification 24, 59, 69
Gill, B. 71
Gopalan, M. 121
Gorski, P. 30
governance structures in schools 68–69
Great Lakes Equity Assistant Center 139
Green, Terrance L. 73, 139
Green v. County School Board of New Kent County (1968) 41
Griffin v. County School Board of Prince Edward County (1964) 44
Gun-Free School Act (1994) 119
Gwynne, J. 61, 71

Hart, C. M. D. 130
Hartford Public Schools 50–51
Hate at School (2019 report) 1
high-stakes accountability 42
Hinojosa, D. G. 106–107
Hispanic Education Act 107
Houston: impact of school closures 60; more school police officers than counselors 108
Hurricane Katrina, state takeover in aftermath of 63–64, 72

Idaho, per-student funding 108
immigration, and population growth 23
Islamophobia 26

Jabbar, H. 47
Jackson, C. K. 108
Jackson, D. D. 8, 9
Jennings, J. 47
Jim Crow laws 115
Johnson, Lyndon B. (President of the United States 1963–69) 80–81
Johnson, R. C. 108
Journey for Justice Alliance (J4J) 62

Kansas City, impact of school closures 60
Kentucky, education as fundamental constitutional right 105–106
Kentucky Education Reform Act (KERA) 1990 106
Kirshner, B. 70
Klein, Joel (Chancellor of New York City Schools 2002–2011) 69
Knowledge is Power Program (KIPP) 121
Kuntz, A. 139
Kyser, T. S. 139

Latinx population growth 23
Latinx students: disproportionate discipline of 118, 120; impact of school closures 16, 59–60, 64, 65, 70–72; impacted by property tax-based funding 102–103; and policing in schools 122; racism against 1; school enrollment increase 24, **25;** segregation in schools 24–25; and voucher programs 44
Lavertu, S. 72
leadership 14; anti-racist school closure strategies 72–74; review in decision-making protocol 146–147;

role in school funding 109–110; school choice 47–51; see also anti-racist leadership
Learning Policy Institute 102
Lee, J. 65, 67
Liddell v. Board of Education of St. Louis (1972) 51
Lindsay, C. A. 130
Lipman, P. 11
litigation, historical context of school funding 100–107
Local Control Funding Formula (LCFF) 102
Los Angeles, California 28–29, 101–102
Louisiana Recovery School District (RSD) 62
Lubienski, C. 65, 67

magnet schools 41, 45, 50–51
Magnet Schools Assistance Program 41
"Make America Great Again" 25–26
Marjory Stoneman Douglas High School shooting 122
market-driven policies, racialization of 10–13
Martin, Trayvon 120
Mattison, E. 117
mayoral appointments in public schools, controversy 69–70
McDonald, Laquan 120
McLanahan, S. S. 125
metropolitan demographics 23
Mexican American Legal Defense and Educational Fund 103
Miami-Dade, more school police officers than counselors 108
Milwaukee Parental Choice Program 44
Minneapolis, Minnesota 29
Morrison, D. 8, 9
My Brother's Keeper (MBK) initiative 8, 27
Myers, L. C. 91

A Nation at Risk (1983 report) 12, 81–82, 85
National Assessment of Educational Progress (NAEP) data 84
National Urban League equity evaluation 89
Nelson, A. A. 121
neoliberal racism 82–83
neoliberalism: agendas and policies navigated by communities of color 73–74; background of mayoral appointees 68–69; bipartisan endorsement of principles in education 59; in education 11–13, 15; of Manor Independent School District Police 122; of *A Nation At Risk* report 81–82; in the No Child Left Behind Act 84; in prisons 115; protocol for combating 138–149; of U.S. government 85
New Jersey, inequitable school funding 104–105
New Jersey Education Law Center 104–105
The New Jim Crow (book) 115
New Mexico Indian Education Act (1972) 107
New Orleans: school choice research 47; school closures 60, 62; state takeover and charter school expansion 62–63, 72, 81
New York City: equitable funding hit by recession 106; mayoral control of public schools 69–70; more school police officers than counselors 108; per-student funding 108
No Child Left Behind Act (NCLB) 2001 12, 16, 28, 42, 59, 80, 81; problems and color-evasiveness 12, 82–86

Oakland, impact of school closures 60

Obama, Barack (President of the United States 2009–17) 8, 26–27, 41, 42, 59, 69, 85–87, 115
Obamacare 86
open-enrollment plans 43
Owens, Jayani 125

parents: activism by 73–74; Black student majority schools and behavior of white parents 45; created non-profit to protect educational rights, New York 106; demographics used in diversity map 49; filed lawsuit against Edgewood Independent School District 102–103; involvement in decision-making 146, 147; and school closures 15–16, 58–59, 60, 61–62, 67–68, 71; as stakeholders in assessment development 91; stereotyped perception of Asian students by white parents 31
Parents Involved in Community Schools v. Seattle School District No.1 (2007) 39
Pence, Mike (Vice President of the United States 2017–) 46
per-pupil funding 101, 104
Persico, C. 108
Pew Charitable Trust 61
Pew Research Center 23
Philadelphia: impact of school closures 60, 67; state takeover and charter school expansion 62–63
Picower, B. 12
policing: of Black and Brown people 27; in schools 122–125
policy analysis tools 17, 139
politics 9–13; behind school closures 68–70; discourse about white supremacy 25–27; of school choice 46; of school discipline 119–120; of school funding 99; and standardized testing 80–90

population growth 23
Positive Behavior Interventions and Supports (PBIS) 17, 126–127
Pozzoboni, K. 70
prison, as destination after school *see* school-to-prison pipeline
Professional Standards for Educational Leaders (PSEL) 4, 110
Project Prevent 126
property tax-based school finance systems: California 101–102; New Jersey 104–105; Texas 102–104
Proposition 209 anti-affirmative action policy (California) 28
Proposition 227 language policy (California) 28–29
Proposition 13 property tax freeze (California) 102
public school enrollment, demographic changes 24–25, **25**

race neutrality in policy implementation 28–29
Race to the Top program (2009) 12, 42
racial achievement gap 29, 42, 82–83, 84, 85
racial context of decision-making protocol 143–144
racism: and color-evasiveness 30; educational inequity 1–2; ERASE framework to identify racial bias 91; hate incidents in schools 1; inherent in school closures 63–68; neoliberal racism, defined 82; against President Obama 86; and President Trump 26; protocol to address systemic racism 138–149, 139–149; and school discipline 115–128; systemic racism in school funding 97–101; uncovered by youth participatory action research 129; *see also* anti-racism, definition; anti-racist leadership

Rallis, S. 139
Rausch, K. M. 119
Reagan High School (RHS), Texas 73
Reagan, Ronald (President of the United States 1981–89) 25–26, 81–82, 85, 115
Reagan, T. 139
recession (2008) 16, 106
regional equity plans 51
response to intervention (RTI) 17, 126
restorative discipline 127
Rethinking Discipline campaign 126
Rhee, Michelle (Chancellor of District of Columbia Public Schools 2007–2010) 69
Ritter, G. W. 120
Roberts, John (Chief Justice of the United States, 2005–) 39
"Robin Hood" plan 104
Rodriguez, Demetrio 102–103
Rose v. Council for Better Education (1989) 105–106
ross, k. m. 6
Rossman, G. 139
rural demographics 23

Safe Passage community escort program 66–67
San Antonio Independent School District v. Rodriguez (1968) 100, 102–103
San Antonio, Texas 28, 29
Schneider, M. 45
school choice 15; benefiting white families 38; and color-evasiveness 39; educational leadership 47–51; equitable options 48–51; inequality and segregation 38–39, 44–46; the market-driven agenda 40–44; policies 37–38; politics of 46
school closure 15–16; anti-racist leadership strategies 72–74; and charter school expansion 61–63; and color-evasiveness 60–63; intersection between geography and race 64–65, *66;* political decision-making 59–60, 68–70; racial repercussions 63–68; racialization of reasons 58–59; research limitations 70–72
school enrollment numbers, diversity of 24–25, **25**
School Improvement Grant (SIG) program 59
school shootings 119, 122
school-to-prison pipeline 17, 115–118, 122, 126, 128, 129
Scott, J. 12
Scriarra, D. 107
segregation of schools 24–25, 40–41; and charter schools 49–50; and magnet schools 50–51; in Minnesota 29; and regional equity plans 51; the role of school choice 38–39, 43; and school closures 63, 67; and school discipline 121; school district secession by white families 30–31
Serrano v. Priest (1971) 101–102
Servoss, T. J. 124
Shanker, Albert 42
Sheff v. O'Neill (1996) 50
Singer, A. 23
Skelton, S. M. 139
Skiba, R. J. 116, 119
social emotional learning (SEL) 127
social welfare cuts in Clinton's presidency 27
Southern Poverty Law Center (SPLC) 1
St. Louis: diverse-by-design charter school 50; impact of school closures 60; regional equity plan 51
standardized testing 16; color-evasiveness of 12; under No Child Left Behind Act 82–86
state takeover, and charter school expansion 62–63
Stovall, David 73–74, 74

Strauss, V. 12
suburban demographics 23
Swann v. Charlotte-Mecklenburg Board of Education (1971) 41

Tea Party movement in Obama's presidency 26–27
teams, working on decision-making protocol 140–143
Texas: disproportionate discipline of Black students 118; education policies 28, 29; inequitable school funding 102–104; policing in schools 118, 122; school closure campaign 73
Three Strikes law 27, 115
transportation to school 45
trauma-informed practices 127
Trump, Donald (President of the United States 2017–) 25, 26, 46
Turner, E. O. 47

Urban Institute 63–64
U.S. Commission on Civil Rights 116
U.S. Department of Education 25
U.S. presidencies: Johnson Administration 80–81; Reagan Administration 81–82, 85, 115; Clinton Administration 27, 115; Bush Administration 28, 59, 82, 84–85; Obama Administration 8, 41, 42, 59, 69, 86–87, 115; Trump Administration 46

Voices of Youth in Chicago Education (VOYCE) 129–130
Voting Rights Act (1965) 80–81
voucher programs 15, 37, 40, 43–44, 43–45, 61

War on Drugs 115
Warren, C. L. 139
Weaver-Hightower, M. B. 28
Wells, A. S. 42
white fragility 4–5, 120
white supremacy 4, 10, 12, 25–27, 115
White Women, Race Matters: The Social Construction of Whiteness (book) 7
Whiteman, R. S. 139
whiteness: catered to by disciplinary solutions 128; definition 4–5; folklore of 26; mistakes permitted under rubric of 131; President Obama appealing to 27; as property 30–31
Williams, N. T. 116

Yazzie/Martinez v. State of New Mexico (2014) 106–107
Young, M. D. 139
youth participation 129–130

Zamarro, G. 71
zero tolerance policies 16–17, 118–120, 122, 129
Zimmer, R. W. 71